Hello to all my exes Copyright © 2023 by Sheryl Ewe. All rights reserved.

No portion of this book may be used or reproduced in any manner whatsoever without written permission except for the use of brief quotations in the context of book reviews.

Printed in the United Kingdom
First edition 2023

Book design by Sheryl Ewe

ISBN (paperback) 978-1-7392061-0-9
ISBN (hardcover) 978-1-7392061-1-6
ISBN (ebook) 978-1-7392061-2-3

Published by Orchid Flower Press
Author Website www.sherylewe.com

This is a work of fiction. Names, characters, places and incidents either are the products of the author's imagination or are used fictitiously. Any resemblance to actual persons, living or dead, businesses, companies, events or locales is entirely coincidental.

To life
cause you're so short

My parents didn't approve. That I was sleeping with an older man. Old enough that he was twice my age, and twice as likely to know that cooking me dinner – with *two* courses (to show he tried) – would canoodle me into bed.

I couldn't help it. I couldn't bear to waste my youth away and I caught him glancing at me at the office, where I sat in the corner, near the office pantry. Bright eyed, overdressed in heels, the intern.

He was walking to the elevators and it was just a glance, so quick, you could barely see it.

Blink once, and it's gone.

But I saw – and that was enough.
Our tongues met furiously in the elevators. Hot and searching. My hands buried in his hair. His hand grabbing my left breast with the audacity and experience only an older man would have. Or maybe only a white man would have.
I still wonder.

Am I a woman yet? Am I experienced?

We settled into an easy rhythm
I brought in my youthful perspective
For I was not yet jaded
In fact, barely broken in
He bought me experience

Paid for by my tight cunt

How would I know that I have one? Because he would tell me, whilst fucking me, all the while moaning and gritting his teeth.

Probably the best fucking fuck he ever had. Just because of my petite size.

Thinking back

I was basically a prostitute – albeit without the actual fistful of dollars left by the bedside table – but I fit the part too

Young, impressionable Asian with long hair and a slender body. Like a willow tree.

With an older, white, man. Did I say white?

I definitely wasn't paid enough.

When we went on holiday, people would stare. Just for a while. As it wasn't too out of the ordinary, seeing a young oriental girl draping off the arm of an older Western man. But they would look nonetheless, a quick glance, raised eyebrows disappearing under their fringe. They judged with their eyes, whilst staring pointedly away. Looking anywhere but me – the ground, the quaint tourist temple, the watch he was wearing. And then they'd pass us, and when our backs were against them, they'd use low furtive voices to debate, to try to make out where I was from, where he's from, what's the age difference, did he find me in a bar, where I was working

During these instances,
I would try to speak louder

Without seeming too conspicuous
But enough to demonstrate my flawless English verse
Without any remaining tints of my previous life as a bar girl –
because I was never one – but my dark hair and slightly tanned skin would always scream so
And condemn me to a sweeping generalisation of Vietnamese women from the war, Thai girls at beer gardens and geishas from Japan – that damn Hollywood movie.
Damn you Rob Marshall.

I have a law degree
Well, I didn't then
But I do now
First Class Honours actually
He didn't even get that when he studied it
But why does it matter
Because he can wear his skin prouder than any degree, badge of honour or trophy
That, my friends, is the single-handedly most lucrative prize of the century
Whiteness
And he won the lottery ticket for that

Anyways, where was I?
Ah yes, I remember. Narrating my promiscuous days, whilst in a mature, monogamous relationship. A quid pro quo.

Our mistress lined his pockets in the form of credit cards. They lounged in his slim leather wallet (the stupid kinds that didn't have any room for anything else, like coins or photographs); a precautionary security blanket
    for the two of us

    My dinners were always taken care of
    Accompanied by wine
    Fundamentally important
    Especially with crushing student debt and measly intern pay (I'm kidding, I was paid for in experience)
    It's not easy to drink fine alcohol – especially out of thin stemmed glasses with deep bowls – almost like a round fish bowl or the full moon in May
    Instead of in barely washed cups, scooped up from and found in the littered, shared apartment's (note: singular) sink –
    The kind where you have to stack, soap and rinse in the same place.
    It was:
    No more Sauvignon Blanc for me
    That was reserved for the basic bitches from secondary school in senior year
    I enjoyed chilled Chardonnay
    And watching
    Its beads of sweat trailing down the outer rim of the glass
    A relatively inexpensive wine (also pretty basic if we're being honest), but oh so versatile and when it's cool and crisp and it hits that right spot

Why then you're floating
And floating
A feather aloof
And the sex becomes enjoyable
Because you're so buzzed anyways
And comfortable from food
That you're smiling with your eyes closed
A cheesy smile like an upturned banana, without showing your teeth
And after that
You could even let him spoon you
So that the two of you could pretend that this – all of it – is solid and secure
And that it won't shatter to pieces
Like a snow globe
Dropped
By an infant child

It's strange
Thinking about relationships
And how most adults seem to fuck theirs up
When *they're* adults
And they spend half of their lives as adults
Telling children not to fuck up their own life
Yeah,
It's strange

I enjoyed telling him I didn't feel like it
On certain nights
Wielding the little power I had
I'd see his eyes harden slightly
Behind the cool exterior
Straighten his face before performing reverse psychology, a customary speech.

"If you wish," he'd say, "of course I won't force it on you. You're eighteen after all. You can make up your own mind."

Other times he'd say, "But you're *young* mon Cher, so full of life, you're meant to want to fuck like bunnies. I thought all people your age did." He'd pout and push me more dessert.

It didn't matter if he ran his lines with words or actions. They were all carefully controlled, so as to give me control.
The pretence of it anyways.
He did it well
Expertly so
Might as well quit his full time job as a senior professional support lawyer to become a full time manipulator.

Oh wait, that's already in the job scope

***

I remember once
Catching him
Take a photo of me
When I was in the shower

He didn't mean to be caught
But I did catch him
He tried to pretend he was unabashed
And even tried to
Weasel out of
apologising.
I made him delete it
and then double delete it from the deleted box

because I knew
It was a photo
For him to keep
Like a prize
and I knew
that we wouldn't last
And I didn't want
To be a hidden token
In someone's phone
Private folder
Hard drive
frozen

as an eighteen year old
In the shower
to be taken out every

once in a while
to admire
and masturbate over
and hung out to dry
like linen on a clothing line
waiting for the sun

also,
it wasn't a very flattering photograph

***

It is always very fleeting to glimpse insecurity in an older man
He didn't look old for his age
In fact, he was rather handsome
Even my mum said so when she first met him
(I had introduced them before he started fucking me)
He had a big cock
Big in a way that I didn't like
I wasn't enamoured by it truthfully, if we're being honest
It was big and chunky in width
                              (so in other words, girthy)
I wanted a long, athletic one

One that would hit my G-spot and make me cum, erupt in the spine, and tingling 'oh Gods',
    arched back and all
    His, would feel good originally

    But after half an hour...forty-five minutes...an hour...
    It wouldn't
    In fact, it felt like a train ramming the insides of a hollowed tunnel
    And I'd have to rush to the bathroom
    Stand there, face red and sweating, dousing myself with a faucet pointed upwards
    Praying for the water to take the heat away
    He gifted me
    thrush
    The first man to do so

    With his fat diameter of a penis.
    I'll say it again.
    My remuneration was unfair.

    I should have demanded a pay raise and fortified my will when I went on strike
    Dressed like a miner
    I should have smeared more dirt on my cheeks and held my ground
    Instead

    I would untie my bra and shimmy down my knickers and acquiesce

    Because this is what all good girls do

    Smile (bite their lip, look up and through their eyelashes) and acquiesce

    I practiced my finishing noises alone
    When he was out at the gym

———

    But what he didn't have down there
    He made up for with his tongue

He'd splay my legs

And start slowly

He began with closed eyes (which boys, you should never do)

And then would pick up the pace

And do things

I don't even know

It certainly wasn't circles

But it made me unravel

And fall to pieces

Like a flower

Plucked

Its petals

One by

One

There was once
We were in Vietnam
(Because when you're in Vietnam)
He went down there
And I almost died
I was clenching and releasing and coming apart
And I wanted to feel him
Everywhere and nowhere
And all at once
I think I cried
My tears segueing into soundless, noiseless, breathless pants

slowly, slowly, I told myself
Pull yourself together
Never let yourself be this bare
In front of a man

Afterwards
I thanked him
and then had to suck his penis
To return the favour.

I made lots of gagging sounds
Just to make him happy

He tried to do the tenderly thing
Taking the strands of my hair away from my face

As if he were my father doing so after my first bike fall with grime on my cheeks, when I flew over the handles after I was able to balance on two wheels – a miraculous feat. I was flying, flying, and then I wasn't and had a face full of dirt.

Just like now, how I had a face full of cock.

And I could see his veins throbbing
And his colour in bright pink, almost red
Erect
Excited and pumped to be there, to be part of it, as if it had just done several reps of weights. Vigorous; a college art student's enthusiastic and messy mix of shades: coral, magenta, rouge and carnations
At least he was respectfully trimmed and shaven
So that his pubic hair wouldn't irritate my nose and eyes

I think I'm pretty good at giving head
For his circumference alone, I deserve an A*.

***

Back to me:
(This is an exercise that my therapist wants me to do. I'm forced to try to feel more comfortable in asserting my presence – just as a male does and doesn't think twice about, which is exactly what makes the exercise redundant when I try to explain myself).

I think this is very personal
But I didn't like his eating me out face
My preference was my ex-boyfriend's
Who had the most handsome face when he was down there

I wish he'd kiss the insides of my thighs more
And start from my ankles
And work his way up
And use that sucking motion thing you do when you want to leave hickeys
And use the tongue to trace
So as to give hot, cold, hot, cold
And then a surprise
In exactly that
Sequenced formation
To leave me flushed and breathless
Saying his name
Apologies, I mean daddy –
He wishes I said it
But I have enough self-control, thank you very much

I admit though
I didn't like anyone going down there at the start
I'd squirm and try to wrestle free
Making stupid snakes on the sheets, as if I was ten and still playing snakes and ladders by myself
It was scary
Unnerving

What if they didn't like it?
What if I didn't like it?
What do I smell like?
Why is it always so much easier to give than to receive
I still find it difficult.
It must be a woman's thing.

Hit over, nailed upon, stapled over and over again to give
 Give when you are pregnant, give when you're awake, give more when you are asleep
 Give until you die
 Your sweat, your milk, your breath
 Your heart
 Always your heart
 Give it
 Away
 Apart
 Together

It doesn't matter. Give it all
Without thanks
Thanks are reserved for fathers who remembered to add a fruit in their kid's lunchbox today

———

I'm trying to touch myself now
Whilst imagining his face
I hope he's wrinkled
And that time has not served him well
Like with John Travolta
And that he has a wife he despises
And kids he hates even more
And so that concludes
My old ex

Because let's be real
I can get myself off with a magic wand vibrator,

quicker too

***

The first time I lost my virginity

I was sixteen

still young

still impressionable

It was raining outside

a detail I remember most out of the encounter

I had always wanted it to rain

when I imagined what my first time would be like

It was sweet

He was older too

I wonder if there is a pattern

Not quite as old as twice my age though

He wore sweaters and leathered jackets

    a disarming smile

    he made me breakfasts

    and left me soon after

    but he liked the quiet when we were together

    said that I reminded him of home.

    it's probably one of the nicest compliments anyone has ever given me

    we used to lie there

    side by side

    barely touching

    one wired earphone in each ear

listening to music
sometimes the rain

it felt romantic

until it wasn't
he gave me perfume
I still use to this day
especially on days that are overcast
and wet
days so dark, they look like night

In London, it's a pretty common occurrence.

the perils of being a woman —
    is another common occurrence

    In a big city
    it's hard to feel safe
    I used to walk home with keys wound tightly in my hand

I remember
    walking behind a young couple, going to work one morning
    I still left enough space between
    our bodies
    but whether it was because of the morning commute
    or because there was the sound of someone simply nearby
    She was the one who looked around —
    not him
    hyper alert
    vigilant
    because this is what it takes to stay alive in this world as a
    woman

    it is not a race issue (they were white)
    it is one of gender

    her partner kept walking along
    oblivious
    still chatting, midstream in his
    sentence

but the girl and me
our eyes met
just locked for half a second
and in that brief moment at 8.30am
we exchanged
mutual understanding
of what it is like
     to walk as a woman
     and breathe.

Is it because I am a woman

That when he kisses my neck
And grips my waist and unbuckles his jeans
I cannot protest
I feel the need
To be stripped down
To match my pace with his
To pretend like I'm enjoying it
And to moan in his ear
Just so it can be over with

For it is easier
         than explaining myself

i don't quite know how to describe it
it is a state of perpetual stress
i feel uneasy in my own skin
i just want to dive underwater
hear nothing else
just the water moving
                and my own breath

it is a hard thing, missing the heat
and longing for it on your skin
it's nice to be in flip flops
and semi-naked
instead of covered in
layers
upon layers
and suffocated with it all

        – my ode to London

In a big city
it's hard to navigate men
"Oh, but I love to watch anime"

you just *know* opening their private browser
will spill only
"Asian girls"
"Submissive Asians"
"Young Asian women"
Any amalgamation of this
in their search history
it's disconcerting
steering through the waters
when the quiet voice in the back of your mind says,

do you like me
for me?

or do you like me
for I look like one of them

or when they do a 180-degree
and tell you
they don't like the colour of your hair
straight, black hair like ebony,
a theatre curtain falling
don't like all girls with this in fact – so it's not *you*, so to speak

but they're fine with
any other colour
blondes, gingers, brunettes
but once they passed a shade too dark, past umber, chocolate,
then it was wading into unfamiliar territory
too black

but they were fine to continue sleeping with you,
of course

———

belittling someone who already feels small is easy

    yes
    i feel like a dandelion sometimes
    that is trodden upon
    and broken
    instead
    i wish i could be cradled in someone's two palms
    whispered to
    and then left alone
    to feel the wind on my cheeks
    my eyes

I've had men:

tell me
"Don't eat your pizza with your hands, we're in a restaurant"
I should have flung it in their face

take me to places where the waiters would ask
still or sparkling
I remember answering once, still please and received a curt laugh after, the firm undertone
"Don't you know? You should have said tap."
"Haven't you ever come to a place like this before?", "Your parents never brought you?"
indirectly telling me
whispering
you are so lucky
that I brought you here

An echo of my past.
It eats me up
like moths devouring the carpets, the silks and cashmere of my home.

I should kill them
the moths.
Before they kill me.

***

<u>Curiosity</u>

Is wanting to be loved
an egoistical thing?

If so, then I am the vainest out there

———

I remember seeing a couple
    They were standing slightly apart
    Waiting for the train or subway
However you want to call it
Depending on what part of the world you're from
And they were both reading paperback novels
separately
silently
But even from the way they stood
I could tell that they were together, an item
I wanted that.
later, I saw them embracing as they continued to read,
    then, they got off the stop before mine

How must it be like?
To move through the world as an individual
Quietly, without taking much space
But with someone by your side,

a unit together

―――――

Maybe I think sex is so beautiful because
when I remove my glasses
the world is just a little bit
messier
a little bit
blurrier
and the shapes and bodies that mould together
look more beautiful,
rounded and softer

blemishes and stretch marks less pronounced.
and best of all

after,
(importantly, *after*) I get to go up close
and stay,
gazing in someone else's eyes
and share a moment of tenderness
that would not remotely be allowed
in other humanely circumstances

imagine doing that normally –
up close,
sharing a moment in the subway with a stranger
or in the bodega downstairs
look deep till you can see their eyes change colour
depending on the light (and how long you stay in that position together)
dark brown to brown, to hints of caramel
if it's blue, then aquamarine to the Croatian Dalmatian sea
feel their breath splay on your nose and cheeks
like a warm Positano breeze
funny how easy it is
to strip down naked, remove all your clothes
for someone you've never met before
and never shared anything with before
and give them a chance
to see you in your most,
vulnerable state

literally
they could stab you
And you'd just die –
naked
ass out
probably with an expression of confusion, bewilderment
kind of bemused

they'd have to bury you with that face

serves you right,

    I told you to only have sex with your friends (whom you find attractive – the types of friends that it's ok if your friendship changes after sex because you were never that close to them anyways, so there's literally nothing to lose and only ascending, incalculable amounts to gain – because it could be the single-handedly best sex of your life, since you already find them attractive anyways and you both know each other – enough to the extent that they'll feel comfortable to reach into the cupboards afterwards to hand you a glass of water – or enough that there is no need for awkward introductions with your flatmates after – like, "yes, this is so and so" – it's more like, "ah NICE," your flatmates would say – without words – in approval, "you got with X, the hot mutual friend of ours" through the exchange of knowing looks,

        cocked eyebrows
        and grins behind cups).

it's fine with strangers
when there are no loose ends –
    what's *not* fine
    is when the sex is so good
    you tell them you love them

    regrettably, this happened before

in all fairness, by that point
    we weren't strangers
    though we would still act like it

we just kept shoving,

suppressing,

pushing,

it

down.

buried it

underneath

layers and layers

of

sarcasm and

non-commitment

stifled it

till vulnerability could no longer breathe

———

A Magic Trick

he pushes up the skirt
revealing the thigh
only for the fingers to vanish
collapse,
             a sigh

***

    we broke the bed before
    it was from IKEA
    and it was hilarious
    we cried laughing, as we fixed it back together
    the parts dismantled
    like Lego pieces
    the kind we bought your cousin for Christmas

too bad you only had eyes for someone else
    and couldn't help it

———

    [aside]

    When we're lying in my bed,
    quiet
    looking at each other, I always wonder
    are you looking at me
    but seeing her?

Blue

Blue is when
your emotions are not your own

and you're sat on a train
watching green flash by
the pictures blurred
blurred
of rolling hills,
and watercolour skies,
curling smoke piled atop chimney roofs,
like whipped cream swirled on crumble pie,

or foam, making love to the stormy ocean
its perfumed pollution.
chased by the musky orange of daylight
the fires – in the distance
tossing
swaying
the slow rumble of the train,
grinding the earth
as you roll by
and watch, your quiet eyes lingering,
hesitating
still
on the blanket of the sleeping countryside.

***

    when we were at the beach

    with the setting sun and crashing waves

    I had never seen you that happy or light, I wanted to see it more

    you kept asking questions

    like an inquisitive young boy

    a load
    lifted off
    of you

    when we slept at night, it was an insight to what it would be like to be married to you

    smiling, with the duvet to our chins

    feet warming

    against

    the winter chill

———

    I pressed a kiss into his palm

    and with it

    gave him my heart

    and told him

    be careful

        because I love you

there's that instinctive trust
so much so you could fly

— Plato's Symposium

———

never have you felt this assurance
this steadiness in a whole person.
never have you felt so
you.

———

and being together is like breathing
easy
natural
you need it to survive
but you don't notice each breath
inhaling and exhaling
it's just instinctive
to function
come alive

the way he grabs me by the nape of my neck
kisses me roughly on my ankles, my calf, the insides of my
thigh
the crook of my neck
my face
presses his lips firmly against mine
opens my mouth with his

    i die

———

    i wanted to hold him
    my child
    to protect him
    and rock him gently
    i'm sorry
    i'm sorry
    let me protect you
    and keep you safe

        i wanted to
        gather him in my arms
        all of the broken pieces
        and hold them
            even if they cut me

                – glass shards

***

After

"You are no longer a unit," my parents said.
"You have to think about yourself," my friends said.
"It's not you and him anymore," my sister said.
"No more sacrifice"

but we grew up together
and the feelings don't just erase
we built our identity around each other
and there's so much care

you just gotta switch it off
but I can't
nothing works
nothing makes sense
i'm sitting here
just sitting here
and
my head
is reeling
spinning
                unmoored

plagued with indecision
fighting to stay afloat
every small decision
feels big

it is
difficult to keep breathing

for days
literal weeks
it is eons before it breaks
that
it's no longer the two of us
just me

    it's cold

some days are easier
Most aren't
I cry alone in bed sometimes
It's been four months

Loving you was the only thing that was easy to me

and so it begins
days like this
lots and lots of
days like this

you put it off
for as long as you can.

hesitate
to say it out loud:
"We're not dating anymore"

for doing so
finalises it
Puts a full stop.
and validates it

In stone

***

after a breakup
I like to mend my heart by
going to the grocery store
I like being sad there
blending in
with the rest of the sparse crowd
No one knows if you're sad when you're at the grocery store
you're just doing your weekly shopping
and there is no time limit
no one to tell you to go away from picking which can of soup to drink
no one to ask whether you need help (because no one cares)

it's wonderful

you can loiter around the gluten free aisle
to secretly hope
that you will bump into any other guy (who is hopefully and miraculously more attractive)
to see if they too suffered from IBS
and maybe they will fall in love with you right there and then
on the spot
at a Tesco

***

After my breakup
I stared hard at people's faces

Hoping they would fall in love with
me
Willing them to

make *me* fall in love with
them

make me forget
him
and make the hurt go away

it's not easy

it's as if you're dying
if I can say so, without sounding too melodramatic

later
it turns into anger,
for placing the wrong chips
down

angry for how it turned out this way
angry at yourself
at him
at the world

it still doesn't make sense

I felt the chasm grow wider and wider

we sat apart
in the cinema
with mutual friends as human body barriers between us

it was dark
but even in the dark
I could tell which one was your breathing

———

i feel every heartbeat
beats out
i miss you
i miss you
as if it doesn't hurt

Is it bad
that I switch off the lights when I'm with him
Because I don't want him
to see me
And I don't want to

see him
because I know he's not you
and I don't want his eyes on my body
because it was yours

as you were
mine

***

I kissed him fast
and fierce
his name nearly slipped from my tongue
    the one who actually mattered

***

breakups are hard
for a long time, I didn't want anyone else

I felt unnerved by other gazes
other penises made me want to
gag

    in the end
    Walks cured my heartbreak
    Walks, alone
    When it's wet
    When it's dry
    In the dark of night
    To work
    To the store
    To see your friends
    Friends are crucial
    Good girlfriends
who can take you out and shove you against another warm body

  keep repeating the motions
  till the hubbub of laughter, conversation, music
  is no longer
      confused

***

In that moment, I was choosing myself
It's not our journey anymore
It's mine

———

green fields
Open space unbounded
I could feel my lungs filling up
and expanding
Like a hot air balloon

[time always helps]

not necessarily cures

but it's a start

then dawn breaks

the first glimmer of spring
after a long winter

***

I like stepping out
    Legs all shiny
        and new
In a skirt that hugs my waist
and kitten heels
Feeling like:
"Watch out"
[Unidentified city]
I'm here
I will conquer you today
I will somehow make 450k
to finally purchase my own one bedroom place
    preferably in a good neighbourhood
    With thick walls
    Ample space for a double bed
    And a chair/sofa to drape my clothes over

so that I can masturbate in quiet and peace
without anyone hearing
least of all my neighbours

...my entire generation is fucked

———

but what can you do?

"Set everything on fire"

everything already is on fire anyways

(global warming is real kids)

      stay in school

Fuck this shit. We're all slaves to the system

the zombies of my mind
    they crowd around and
    stare
    with huddled scarfs
    blank eyes
    pinched heels and sore ankles
    tired shoulders, full bellies
    starving for some open space
        the freedom of life

***

If I dive underwater, I can't hear them and they can't hear me

***

    the sakura were blossoming
    It was May
    they floated

    graceful,
    as they fell
    to their deaths

***

I look at her sometimes

eyes tired, hands worn
and try to imagine her
in my place
in my spot
at my age

how were things like?
what were your dreams mama?
were you like me? or more importantly,
      am I like you?

are you proud of me
as I am of you?

I'm sorry I hurt you sometimes
I don't mean to

Your sacrifices are incomprehensible
even when I sit
  and try to imagine

           – mama

you put aside your dreams
to let us live ours.
we were your dream
but were we worth it?

                                    i don't think so

———

my mother likes to read my writing

a trait she's learned since my younger days
when I was ten and she read my diary
the one with a dolphin on it
there was no lock, cause I found those fiddly
and she found out I had a crush on a boy in my class
we were on the swim team together
it was only natural I liked him

                             (when he swam butterfly
                                 he skimmed the water
like a pebble skipping, or a dragonfly darting across the surface of
                                              a pond)

it was horrible
I went ballistic
especially since we were late to meet him by the poolside
she reads more than my writing.

To this day
my mother can still read me
she always knows when I'm infatuated
even though I've gotten pretty good at hiding it
I've changed my tactics over the years
stopped smiling at my phone so much
refrained from speaking too much (about that particular person)
abstain from speaking overall, lest I give it away

she'll always ask me point blank
do you love them

she's consistent, my mother
she still reads my work
in an attempt of failed secrecy

why I caught her reading this

———

my mother and I,
when we go through her jewellery box together
I get a glimpse of how things were like when she was younger
she enjoyed variety
different gems for different days, summer or overcast
she bought many herself
because who will treat you better than you?
she has a skin tone that makes gold precious

―――

    my mother and I, we are the same size
    I have a fondness for all her clothes
    the ones with the stiff shoulder pads
    and 80s print
    block pencil skirts and
    high-waisted jeans
    flare anything with
    ribbons for her hair

she had beautiful hair when she was younger
    it's easy to see why my dad fell in love with her
    she was elegant and polite, most of all
    patient

    many traits I'm not

    luckily, I can fit into her clothes

―――

Her cream puffs are heaven
    fluffy and light
    sweet, but not overboard
    I'd plunge the whole spatula in the bowl and lick it,
    devour it whole

―――

my mother cries when she sees me hurting
the most recent was when both of our heads shared a pillow
in Montreal

she cried when my ex and I broke up
she loved him like her own son

he was like her
gentle and soft spoken
it's not hard to see why they got along

she cried again with my most recent breakup
but this time, she wasn't mourning him
I think she was mourning me

— a mother's love

***

Your mother is the truest love you'll ever know
how do you let go when they pass

"I'm an orphan," he said
Crying to me on the phone

fathers that abuse
leave grown men feeling
small

when they are the opposite of that

———

advice from my mother

Find someone who loves you more
Than you love them
Because as a woman, you end up giving too much anyways

———

my mother
and her sacrifices

even when I was younger
when I had fractured my left arm
they made her hold me
in the X-ray room
they gave her a vest
I wasn't crying
wasn't fussing
but they made her hold me
and withstand radiation
exposure
she asked why.
they said:
you're a mother, you must always
sacrifice

— X-ray

***

one of my ex's mother
once told me she was jealous of me
she felt that her son gave me more love
and she wanted some

said that it broke her heart
every time she saw us hold hands
because she would see
that he was capable of giving and loving

    boys of the world, please shower your mother with love

                            they do too much and us,
                                    not enough

***

I've always been a daddy's girl

it was Sunday and
the cream donut was sliced in quarters
I made my pick and of course, as luck would have it – my selection
didn't have any filling inside
"Life choices," my dad mused, looking at his fork

it was surprisingly deep
for afternoon brunch

my father has always preached about the importance of avoiding
"wrong decisions"
and when I say avoid, I don't mean,
bolt from the laden truck belting down the autobahn
but to plan for the escape in advance
preferably five years ahead
before you even get the driver's licence
preparation is key
he's a project engineer
of course planning is important

he once told me that I should forgive my teacher (who had flown
into a rage – one comparable to a cartoon flying off the walls with
a reddened face and steam whistling from his ears), because he
didn't have sex

my dad frequently repeats this:
an angry driver? didn't have sex
an angry staff member? didn't have sex
angry overall? didn't have sex

forgive them
because they didn't have sex

it always helps to imagine this,

                                      take that you smug bitch

———

my mother
she phrases things differently
she says
You have to walk through society with your choices
Meet and greet peers, companions and others
and justify those choices
If you can do so,
then that's ok
but you must be able to

        it's not easy, wearing her clothes

I remember teaching my parents about self-defence
survival tactics
if anything happens and you need help
Don't scream "help"
scream "fire"

my dad smiled and said
why not scream "I'M NAKED"

This is the same man who taught me self-love

that self-praise is public disgrace

that family always comes first

it has always been easy to talk to my father

———

he told me to have high standards
told me to choose my partner carefully
half-joked that they would need to be good like him
with his character
someone upright
who treats me generously
who has the same affinity
of respect and courtesy
the same values and morality

whose manners are exemplary

not someone who's my contingency

but someone I love profoundly

with tenacity

and tempered tranquility

for the long years ahead

who won't waver through uncertainty

instead undoubtedly

stay

steadfast as stone

consistently

and exclusively

with humility

someone noteworthy

the two of us complementary

it's not easy

when things end with your ex

knowing your father liked him

and welcomed him into the family with extended arms

it's not easy

when your father still wishes the best for him

it's as if he keeps the door unlocked

and unlatched

– a verbal prayer

people say that I look like my father
indeed I am my father's daughter
it has always been easy talking with him
and opening up
easy to see his youth
reflected in his eyes
to have our talks stretch on for hours
into another coffee cup

———

My father
He's a very honest man
He's the type to return a napkin if he's given two

Too bad this morning he turned to me and said,
"have you realised
you don't plan, you stumble"
he's not wrong
        but it still stung

***

I remember seeing
when I took the bus N98 to go to work
a father without fail
would take his young daughter to Hyde Park
he would push her in her pram
and adjust her winter bobble hat to make sure the flaps
would cover her ears
and alight
the whole expansive park in store for her
I would think to myself
What are you up to
What do you do
How lucky she is
to have the whole day with you

– I would watch them through the misty glass

***

He was the type to
Not live his life for himself
But entirely for her

when we lived apart,
I would disembark from the plane and grab my luggage
my mother would be waiting for me
at arrivals

every time I hugged her
she would seem smaller
more petite
her wrists small
I was the one enfolding her
but all at once, in that singular moment, I'd feel small

reduced to a child
it's a scary process, thinking about change

my father would be waiting by the car
so he wouldn't need to park
he'd usher me along
and help me lift my suitcases in the trunk
before likewise wrapping me in his arms

I live for these moments
hugging them

physical touch is my love language

———

I found out recently
that I was a hugger since young
I would cry
whenever there was lightning and thunder
till my grandmother would pick me up
and hold me against her chest

she understood
even when I was only a few months old
that I needed touch and love to survive

———

The fear when you're watching a sunset and you know it's about to
set
you can't bear to watch it sink
and you're getting this feeling of trepidation
because you just want to click pause
and hold this moment,

the sun in your hand

***

[reminisce about your childhood kiss]

I remember being so scared to kiss you
Remember thinking you're Hispanic so you'd know how to kiss
since your mother tongue is the romantic kind

you were so gentle
it was too gentle
as if you'd thought I'd break

---

we used to take walks on the beach
with the sun illuminated on your face
     watch people play football
in jeans

we were young and we didn't know any better
in that stage of life where we neglected friends to hang out more together
you were quiet and tended to speak more with your eyes
but sometimes you were so very far away
I didn't know how to reach you
but maybe, I didn't fully try

our favourite place
was on the couch in grey sweats
our best memory together was in my back garden
that was the first time I let a boy's hands under my t-shirt

you'd tell me about your grandfather's orange tree in the countryside
your eyes distant
I think you'd thrive the best out there – in the stillness

with only nature sounds punctuating the quiet,
growing old with someone

but
we were young, we didn't know any better

when we ate in restaurants together
it felt too grown up,
as if wearing a different skin

we didn't know how to hold ourselves in public
couldn't separate love from lover,
fact from fiction

you had a hardened exterior
one reserved for the outdoors
but you were so soft, behind closed walls
it was like dating someone bipolar

I recall you with fondness
you taught me that unequal relationships don't work out
I'm sorry for breaking your heart

———

You're the kind that gets so invested in love
you end up squeezing them, constricting them
till the love dies

                                        – boa constrictor

———

I think all the quiet ones are the most romantic
    you spoiled me with affection, compliments
and jealousy

not all gifts I wanted

———

everyone deserves someone to dote on them
    and you deserve that too

                                        – happy birthday

***

[think of another]

When I see someone kissing
I think of you
even your very voice would make me want to groan into your
    mouth

crawl into your mouth

seize you by the hair
and taste you whole

it's instinctual
animalistic
a knowing without experiencing
a curiosity to feel your body with mine

I flirt because I want to see you unravel
    quite frankly, we do it well
evenly paced
well matched
enough   space
and tension
in   between

but we don't work well together

better apart

sometimes desire is worth fanning,

but sometimes all we desire
is desire itself

***

Oh darling
How long will we keep this up?
The pretence
The tease

It's the biting of lips
but never tasting
It's the disquiet ease
but never lingering

It's the game we play
of insincerity

but we wrap it up in sweetness
with some vanilla

***

We drank so much wine
Our lips turned blue

I remember it so vividly
Head spinning
Mouth tingling
When I was
Kissing you

***

when I met you, I just knew –
it was like an inescapable pull of the ice cream stand on a
sweltering hot summer's day that made me drift
                                            towards you

    sugar like nicotine
    you being heroin

Young love
is the delighted charge and whoop
of running till the end of the pier
and launching yourself off
into the infinite bask of summer's waters
headfirst

                                              – without fear

———

It was like a scene from a movie
we saw each other from afar
and started running
then we were in each other's arms
in an embrace

                            never let go of something so good

———

I love the kinds of relationships
that afterwards
You're still friends

and you'd laugh over your previous escapades
"Remember when we used to rack up the phone bill"

it's so precious it cannot be fully captured into words
just knowing that you are still loved and cared for
by someone where there *was* mutual love and care before

***

we had the best 'how we met' love story
sat in a pub
in an attempt to make friends
we ended up chatting to each other all night long
instinctive, no one else
we weren't purposely trying to ignore anybody
but we ended up doing exactly that

– pub affairs

***

I'm sorry we didn't work out
But thank you for the memories
I will always love you
And am grateful for your presence in my life

Friends
are
pancakes and proms
sleepovers and pranks
opening the fridge without fear in their home
being on a first name basis with their parents

girls sharing their experiences
common threads of good and bad
shipping essentials across oceans
because you cried on the phone amid your boxes
knowing you needed to iron your clothes for work the next day

neighbours giving you organic vegetables
fresh flowers
toilet paper during a pandemic

boys welcoming you into the fold
to chat on MSN Messenger
about girls they like
to play sports together and lie on a beach talking about life
to support the underdog in a boxing match
to soften, open and
verbalise

friends are love

friends are pain
they are the small gestures to show someone cares
paying for takeaway pizza
accompanying you on mundane tasks
like the dry cleaners and making it fun
or to errands like the doctors
for your pregnancy test

for loving you, even when you're a bitch
friends are
Harry and co.
can you name a more iconic trio?
taking care of your plants when you are away
cooking baby mush when you're riddled with tonsillitis
holding your hair when you're retching

making music videos because there is nothing better to do, nowhere better to go
falling asleep together during a late night film
or laughing till it hurts
and wheezing from re-runs of Friends
drawing on each other's faces with
permanent marker

friends can leave
friends can fade
they are the promises of youth
and another life

    friends are sometimes
                family

sometimes strife

***

    I've witnessed so many close friendships gradually disintegrate. It starts with an earnest promise, "I'll message you everyday," till the days drag on into weeks, and the weeks fade on into years.
    It doesn't always get easier.

***

    let me project my wants and desires
    into the universe
    and hopefully my manifestations come back
    and hit me
    square in the face
    with the full force of a big bang

            – this is how the world began

it is hard accepting sometimes
people moving on
you have this piece of them stored away in your memory
and you want to hold onto it
preserve it in the way you conserved and took care of it all this time
it is hard reconciling that
they can find greater loves than you

———

recognising that you are a bad friend
takes courage

———

I wish I could write letters to my old friends
reminiscent to the yearbook messages you leave at the end of the year
and tell them without judgement
just reception
what I love and hate about them
and how I'm angry they left me behind

the phrase it takes two to tango
is not just for romantic relationships

———

friends are a blip
a moment in passing, while frozen in youth

other times, they are your other self
sitting across oceans

sisters are your first and last best friend

***

our innocence was something to behold
building forts
and pretending the floor was lava
rewinding the VHS tapes, the cassettes
to flip on a movie
the one we rented from the DVD store
karaoke with Britney and Avril
with forks for mics
Papa Johns delivery
extra mushrooms & pepperoni
instant Maggi noodles
and scrambled eggs
deeeeep tubs of ice cream
with only one spoon
screaming at Jurassic Park
at the top of our lungs
midnight strolls
without our parents knowing
leaving footprints in the snow
building things together
an icicle castle
in the deep of night
our quiet lights
rosy cheeks, wide eyes

forging a lifetime of memories
to always remember

who knew, they would be so sweet?
after growing up
and looking back

raiding each other's closets
cocooned under blankets & toys
never-ending conversations, cryptic languages and codes
insecurities bared
a thousand tears shared
secrets buried deep that nobody else knows
not even you sometimes
but your sister,
she dug up
and
unfroze

      – your sister is your protector, she knows you inside out

feel the excitement of
witnessing fresh snow
falling from the sky
it's soft and drifting
with all the promise of the season
yes you can do it
stick out your tongue
you're young
outstretch your arms
spin around
fall down into
that delicious crunch
wave your arms
up and down
synchronised legs
matching crowns
making angels in the snow
because the days lie ahead of you
like a white duvet of potential
and fun

— wintertime snow

You were in it	if you did
living it	would you have tried holding
You didn't think	on more
twice	squeezing it tight
to consider	
that	would you have stopped,
You were actually creating	to sit back and
memories	look,
	try to catch sight?

***

when in Hokkaido
or Sapporo
order your favourite prawn tempura
plunge your spoon into the bowl
again
and again
keep fishing it up
the ramen and the udon
the tastes of your childhood

                                                        – a haiku
                                              [just the nostalgia]

The beads of snow
hung precarious
on the tips of branches,
the ice
thin and drawn out
as a wicked witch's nose
it was beautiful in Russia
the beaches with sand and gravel
and red stones
we used to pretend they were rubies
and we were genies
and Tsars
we walked on frozen seas
a great big slab of ice
stretching as far as one could see
before it would
break
    off in
        smaller chunks
like broken pieces of
mosaic tiles
on the bathroom floor,
we watched them drill holes
and fish for salmon
the ice at least 1 metre thick
their flasks of tea by their side
their faces flushed from cold
and pleasure,
pink
with delight,
    crisp in wintertime

– Sakhalin

***

Can I keep it safe
If I pen my memories onto the page
If I iron them out onto paper
Press them to make them live for an eternity
Even if we can't

– memorialise

***

when the sky is like candy swirls
baby pink and orange
and you think to yourself
I'm so lucky to be alive

– cotton candy

Memorable memories

Lying on a surfboard and screaming to the blue sky
The boys you like and how they don't like you back
Getting money for midnight snacks and candy during sleepovers
Running through wet fields in the pitch of night
Adrenaline up to your throat
Friends shrieking in laughter and scattering in all directions
Because you were all out past curfew
Trespassing and drinking

Your first kiss
And second and third
Anytime you could step into a sea
And submerge yourself in waves

Late nights piled up on a red sofa
With conversations leading to nowhere
Dance parties on tables with bad music
Till the sweat stings your eyes
And the rain falls
A full thunderstorm and you're lying on the grass
Without a care in the world
It's warm and it's wonderful
And you're infinite

Because you're young
And free
And the world is yours for the taking

– your youth

***

He seized me
forceful with his hot mouth
pinned me down with his hips

confused beauty in disorder
the colours of the sky
alight, orange fire bloom

i built my house on shifting sands

***

After moving again for the eighth time in eight years
    I would spend my time on the train
browsing the Instagram of responsible adults
    Rightmove
    the details and filters all saved
(decent size, preferably freehold but at the bare minimum, long leasehold, lower price range)
    cross my fingers
    and imagine a different life
    one where I could, actually browse
    in physical person
    and say "I'm interested"
    be worthy of their time
    an actual contender
    a valuable member of society

    to step in and take a deep breath
    feel that flutter in the chest
    and that feeling
    of being home

***

Home is a strange concept
For me, it has always been found in people

    It gets harder to find it as you grow up
        to secure it
& friends
    who mutually understand
    what it's like to move
    the worries
    fears
    pain
    joy
    the inescapable fact of loss
to experience an entirely different culture
    Where English isn't the main language

I wish I didn't need to explain myself
often/ever
but that's why when we find others like us
    we band together

    today was such a day
    having dinner with a comrade
    who understands its pain

"We're so good together though," he told me
    but to her, moving "it's a holiday"
        to me, "it's a lifestyle"
        to us, it's all we've known
        and all we want

    it's difficult
reconciling your relationship with that

    Her parents not liking him because he's black
        How do you feel ok with that
        How do you remedy that
        How do you forgive that
"I'm no longer in a place where I feel like I can"

    – Biracial couples &
        TCK problems

    So i threw away pieces of my heart
    carelessly
    like i was a child once more
        throwing away petals
            from the flower i just picked

home

        I know it is just a notion, a physicality
            sometimes a dwelling, a place

      but it's hard to let go, harder to give in

you start to forget the familiar smells
the way you can walk blindfolded in the dark
take the stairs two at a time
savour the way the key jingles in the door
the way the door-handle turns
for when you move again
you'll have to re-learn it all
        new pathways
           back lanes
    and people's names to greet in the local store
    new tricks on how to shimmy the lock
so you can do it one-handed with all your bags
    or to dash in before your sister,
because you nicked her stuff without her realising
        and she'll notice soon

    do the handles turn
    or are they the kinds that you simply push
    the worst are the doors that you have to distinctly pull
forward
    before they slam shut

I want my own place so bad
so I can paint my own walls
in any colour I like
         golden
like in the Bridge of Terabithia
            blue or green elsewhere
yellow for my kitchen
each room with a distinctive personality

        to even draw wide brush strokes
    or random scribbles
             on Mondays

hammer in paintings on the wall
instead of measly Blu-Tacking posters
just to peel them off later
do things without landlord ramifications

to set things more concrete
anything,
hell, the bed in the living room

        because it would be mine

***

i feel like our whole generation needs a time out
a good old festival (not that i've ever gone to one, but from what i can imagine or gather from Instagram)
to let loose and breathe

to have ridiculous amounts of mud smeared everywhere
and face paint caked and mingled with sweat
(and i wish glitter, but i guess not, since it kills turtles and the environment)
but otherwise, with
tongues
lots of them
and love
and passion
and companionship

to be young
where mistakes can be made
and it's okay

in fact,
perfectly fucking acceptable

you know what's not okay?
for the fate of the world
to be resting on our shoulders

for the big shots and big names to
point fingers at us
and tell us
"we're so excited for what you'll do next"

no.
take responsibility
you've had your fun, you made this mess
fucking clean it up

stop trying to pass the baton

      for i'll just drop it

           [and no, it's not imposter syndrome,
                i'm just sick of your shit]

<u>let us live our youth</u>

without thinking too much
because thinking
kills
it simmers and festers
in your gut
before reaching up to
strangle
      you in a chokehold

you've fed us all these lies
to which we've swallowed
"study hard, and then you'll be happy"
"get into uni, and then you'll be ecstatic"
"get a job, and then you'll be free"
so then why is there this ceiling that i cannot break?

i've always played by the rules
for the rules to just play me

first class honours
furloughed
booted out of the country that i've forged ties with for seven years
amid friendships
and some semblance of roots

just rip me out from the ground
yank me clean

despite my wishes and wants.
i still have to carry around
a stupid ID card that proves otherwise

couldn't apply to another job
without repercussions
and lengthy 'fill in the <u>blanks</u>'
and forms
of my name, date of birth and address,

multiple addresses — all of them —
of every single place that i've stayed over the years
records and the lack thereof
and sponsorships
for who wants you after all (cause we sure as hell don't)
and guarantors and proof of funds
and proof of nationality, identity, certificates;
the humiliating (dehumanising) list goes on

it all boils down to this single phrase: do you have the right to stay?

no?
well, get the fuck out

i get it
i fucking get it
i'm not one of you
but i'm not one of them either
i'm not one of anywhere
and it's hard
it's hard to be rootless
and spinning
to feel comfort on a plane

knowing you're going on
to the next bit
whatever that is

how can i know what i want
how can i fully
long to stay in a country that doesn't want me
my desires
convoluted
spineless
confused
emotional

it messes with you
and makes you feel old
and everything is so fucking expensive nowadays
why is it so expensive
why can't it be better
and easier
safer

it's infuriating
i'm just constantly
internally crying

let me just spiral down
into the 5.45 x 2.65 inch screen

my face illuminated in the darkness
my thumb
infinite

you can't stop reading the news
so you keep doing it –
all the fucking time
even though you know it messes with your

damn fucking mind
mental state, sanity
the holy trinity
it's hard –
but addictive
to scroll down
        and learn of the horrors of the world

maybe it's a coping mechanism
to match the horrors
of your mind

———

wow, you're like
really angry
[audible sigh]

yeah

if anyone says "coding" or "AI" one more time, I'll rip my ears off
                                            and scream

and the ravages of poverty
caught me
in the sun room
our selflessness,
        self-destructive

              The world is changing.
           too fast
    and yet somehow, not fast enough

I care too much and that is my downfall

        maybe these ramblings will tide me over,
                          but maybe not

— 3 a.m. convos

---

here is my letter of resignation
I'm too tired to continue facing it
an increasingly angry and disagreeable society
    the world in a nutshell

Is it
wrong that
when he flicks his tongue over your nipple
it turns hard

Because to him it's just another breast.
and to you
it's
shivers
    a gasp of vulnerable breath

***

Blue is the strongest intensity
shut up
Don't care what they say –
it's not red
They lie

they lie, or else they've never seen
his blue
his eyes
looking back at yours

***

Things they don't tell you about adulthood
that you have to cook so often
and that you'll savour sleep

that you can buy a full-size lemon drizzle cake *anytime* you want
because no one will stop you
it can be your staple lunch instead
    (as well as ice cream, when there's nothing left in the fridge)

that you have to clean up and wash up
all the time
it's really quite repetitive
why is it so repetitive

how tiring it is, separating your work clothes from your day clothes
and your comfy clothes
and your going out to the corner store "I don't give a fuck" clothes
and the clothes that it's a little bit risky but you're ready for a good time, so you're like "fuck it, might as well"
    chuck it on

how it's fabulous to trail around the apartment naked
and bare
that you can walk from the bathroom, to the living
brushing your teeth

you know what else they never teach you about adulthood?
that if you accidentally lock yourself out without a key
there's really no way of getting back in, except two options
and both end up leaving you looking like an idiot anyways
1) call the locksmith
2) your landlord
3) but really, you should stick to option 1, because you want to
avoid your landlord at all costs (because nobody likes landlords)
and it's a two-way relationship – they ignore you anyways,
even if water is dripping from the ceiling

(I once even offered to paint the apartment for my landlord for free
    just because I couldn't stand the chipped paint and stains.
                  he was ignoring me for weeks beforehand
                              but lo' and behold,
the paint, its roller and tray were found on my doorstep the
                                  very next day)

why wasn't I warned about
how there are different kinds of taxes
income and council tax and GST
that everything costs money
food, water, bills, phone plans, internet, space, air
even locking your bike
you gotta buy locks for your locks
because thieves are gettin' really greedy these days

I suppose they too are suffering from inflation

timing
is so important
even the very best of relationships
can die because of it

***

He kissed me with
ferocity,
velocity in which
my clothes dropped to the floor
and lay abandoned to next morning

———

He was obscenely beautiful
with dark lashes and dark hair
a look that could eat you whole
and keep you safe
        simultaneously

He'd wear dark jeans and a white T
and you'd catch yourself staring

lingering too long

the first night I met you
we climbed through your window to get to your bedroom
like burglars
cause you forgot your key

———

we cycled together
in all the different neighbourhoods
east and west, rich and poor
sometimes with me perched on your handles
sometimes side-by-side on the pavement

you taught me how to avoid the red buses
shouted at the taxis that honked us
marvelled at the way the wind blew our hair childlike

we were free together
chasing twilight
and sunsets
and city lights down by the Thames

the wind bit us when we didn't wear jackets
but we didn't care
we flew instead
our beams planted on our faces, freedom stretched from ear to ear

this was our piece of London
everyone should have at least one summer
of being invincible

———

I thought chivalry was dead
till you came along
you would pick me up from work
and drop me off
take the bus with me
just so we could spend more time together

you made me torta della nonna, before our first date
it was as if you instinctively knew, I adore all sweet things
you even bought dessert packaging
just so it would be presentable
instead of serving it in a
plastic container

we sat under a tree
near work and ate it together
afterwards, I had to lie to my boss and say it was from
the bakery nearby

at night
when you waited for me by the tube
I remember just *feeling*, my heart pounding in my ears
and my cheeks flushed from the cold
and you looked so handsome
hair wet from the rain
resting on your bike

I remember thinking
I must have been very good in my past life

I will keep it as a memory,
close to my heart

———

                                        your eyes are always quiet in the morning
                                              you like to watch more than you speak

———

I love your hands
They are a sculptor's hands
A lover's hands

– you're a quiet man

———

                                                      You were always one
                                                         To hold a gaze

Green eyes flecked with brown
Framed by eyelashes longer than dreams
Lips curved
And dipped just the way I like at Cupid's bow
He was so pretty
It was unworthy
For him to walk down the street
or do something mundane like groceries
He made breathing a new hobby for me to admire
He made walking something
for me to soften

His laughter made me weaken
without any accord

He was what made birds sing
and the sun to peek out each day
He had forearms that I wanted
Wrapped around me
For that's the only way they should be
With his natural veins
Like tree roots and branches stretching across his skin
Life growing
at his lips

***

My cheek would fit
Into the crook of your shoulder blades
like a glove
Cradled like it was chiselled there on purpose
For the onlookers to gaze upon
And wonder

Titled: love

***

Our tongues met
and greeted in the same language
we were naturals speaking and conveying
our emotions and passions
we understood each other
in hurried fashion
our mind-reading so clear – it was instinctive,
and the communication of our tongues caressing
was quite frankly, addictive

— mutual languages and mother tongues

we'd go and eat ramen
and chicken
in that small shack by Tottenham Court Road
it was so romantic that
I'd fantasise about us in Japan
blowing away the steam from our bowls
gazing at the golden temple in Kyoto
nibbling mochi ice cream
and dawdling in stores
everything looking so kawaii

delighting in how it all tastes so fresh
even the air
on your tongue
and skin
your lips tasting like miso and rice green tea

a polaroid of us in front of
Mount Fuji

– our ramen place

Ribbon

legs intertwined
and heartbeats slowed
he traces your lips with his tongue
slowly,
slowly, you unravel and
become undone

lips stained with kisses
breath, hot in your ear
fingers,
fumbling fingers
        combine together, then unwind

———

We had London licking from the palm of our hands
Frozen like a silent snow globe
Instead of its usual deafening din
The roar of the streets
Replaced by the quiet
        of your arms

we spent all summer hunting
for blue plaques

Lenin in Bloomsbury,
Yeats in Primrose,
Dame Agatha in Cresswell Place,
you humoured me
taking photographs of great men and women
marvelling at their deeds

Turing in Maida Vale,
Gandhi as a law student,
Dylan Thomas in Camden
        and Virginia too
Some had lived there and died there, which was quite frankly,
        humbling

Sir Lawrence repose in Grove End
Benjamin Britten and Peter Pears amid the woods
Emily Davies championing, in Cunningham Place
you noticed a false exterior on the ornate.
        Mid-Victorian terrace,
        Bayswater's unbroken façade

        a non-existent place, on an existing street
        it was the beginning of our habit,
        to intersperse truths in lies

                – plaques & cracks

We can't save each other
When we are drowning ourselves

———

In him
I see a whole other person sometimes
someone unstable, ready to
Blow

he had that sort of personality
where he'd give food to a dog
and then days later
when the stray kept coming back
he'd say
I can't pet him
why?
Because I'll leave and
I don't want him to die of a broken heart

———

    I'd hug him sometimes
        in an attempt to fix something so starved and broken

———

        but wounds fester when they are left to sit, for too long

        someone you see
        whose pain is so deep

        how do I reach you?
        how do I help you?

please
        don't shut down
        don't shut me out

I'm sorry I'm sorry

                ***

        here's some silence

        [Blank page]

Sometimes I think about the time when you first saw me
Did time slow down for you
What caught your eye
The way I smiled?
I wonder if it is etched,
in your brain
And if it burned a hole
Do you remember the pattern on my dress
The colour of my hair, from afar
How my hand extends
How it felt in yours
when we shook in greeting
Did you fall in love with me
And never want to let go

                              I have a good handshake

– our first meeting

***

spring is
the first buds flowering
the rains still coming
but lighter
more gentle, subdued

its puddles not deepening,
instead shallowing
coats swapped out for cardigans
for walks under elderflower trees, blossoming

blues fainter,
more watercolour than acrylic
skies more muted than vibrant
but with the promise of new beginnings

– spring bloom

I could imagine quiet days with you
a house with a garden and lawnmower
a life free from worry and stress
there was no need to strive for greatness
just a beach with a moon and red sand
an apartment with clean bedding and furniture in Valencia
good food and simple meals of meat and polenta
days spent lounging in each other's arms

there would be no need for something else
I could just stay and be myself

— remain

***

He seized her and together they tumbled
Over the mound of grass
His actions playful
The night sky open and bare
She had never felt like this
The rush of the sea air
He leaned over her
Her breath quickened
His lips drew closer
This is what people are always talking about

— it was November

I sometimes think about escaping

how we could have runaway to live in tents
with the open plains before us
for you to go back to your beginnings
and for you to bring me back

to the steppes
with the wind whistling through our hair
our cheeks reddened from the cold and sun
the grass under our feet in soft wool

could you have opened up your heart more
could you have accepted my ways
I don't think I would have been bored
not with you anyways
not if we could have stayed, wrapped up naked in each other's arms
running free on horseback
not if we could have been swimming in glaciers and lakes
our smiles free like sunsets

wider than horizons
larger than bare skies stretched across mountain plains
not if I could feel your lips and tongue
forever sweeping across my everglades
tracing down my neck, hot and wet
inserting within

free me
teach me your ways

       jumping off into clouds
           free falling into your arms

           I could descend into darkness
             just to chase this feeling

                euphoria and adrenaline
                   your name on my lips

***

I think it's cause you blew air in my lungs
and made me feel
like I could run,
run hard
for miles, thousands of miles
dart across a glade like a gazelle with infinite bound
oxygen in my bloodstream
so pure and high it was absorbed by skin

you made me feel that way
like there was no other way of living than this

                                          – full lungs

I could feel my yearning
swelling for you
like a tidal force
and how my waves continued to break
in rapid surfs
against the shore

– Vale of Glamorgan

***

throw your leg
over the crumbling wall
say a prayer
between the kissing gate
squelch in your Wellies
slip in the mud
admire the sheep
and the coastline sea-rush
feel the salty breeze
skip against your cheeks
feel them whisper
your name
take it far out to sea
hear it dangle
– your being –
murmur through
floating branches of trees

– coastal path walks

touching
and ducking
hiding and mucking
venturing out to play
a quick embrace before
twirling and spinning away

our tongues collided
and swooped
like the crescendo of a
           spilling wave

they followed each other naturally
    like how the crest follows gravity
        and tumbles down
           the face of a wave

              – our dance duet (a pas de deux)

***

      Your mouth burst with song
      Like melody to my lyrics

you would trace the outlines of my lips
like waves greeting the limestone cliffs
just as inevitable
during high tide

                               — Wales

***

Have you ever had that moment
Where you wanted to reach into the screen
And snog his face off

— fingers around the nape of his neck

***

you pried me open easily
made me weaken
my legs spread out of their own accord
it's not like I needed any teasing

nor was I hesitant
there was not so much as
a glimmer
of caution or care
versus one prying open a new book
with hesitation and fear

                the pause

before the
careful ease,
the slight shimmy
of its plastic cover –

the admiring
before the uncovering,
the hovering
before the discovering,

with a spine that had not yet been yawned
                              to stretch –
        for the very first time
for its initial owner

I did not tread carefully
with heed
I was only urgent
to feel you inside of me

                        – flushed cheeks, pounding heartbeats

the fields were not green
they were brown and flowering
like wheat mills all around us
coming up to our waist as we ran through them
hand in hand
making new paths and streets

the sun was glorious
it made my black hair shine copper and brown
our skin flawless
in summer glow and magic

our corneas burning bright
our irises speaking of affection
and lust
mostly lust
of youth
our summertime

why does foreplay feel so good

                    is it
the wondering

                              before the mustering
the fluttering

                              before the shuddering

            or is it the
              usher of
                  ecstasy

                            the trembling

                          before
                          the
                          immersion
                          of
                          heavenly

                                – foreplay

I loved his hands
not for the way they looked
but for what they could do

how they would make me tremor
   a giant quivering

      an earthquake
on Richter scale 20
instead of 10.

      – a giant orgasming

***

   all I wanted to do
   was to put my fingers in his mouth
   behind his teeth
   to pry them open
   like a hook on a fish line

   to pull him towards me
   for an open mouth kiss

      – hooked

Was it sexual tension
Or frustration
We were shoving each other
Tripping over our laces
Knew it had to be in secret
Our interludes
And meetings

I remember us
>   *pretending*
that we were only friends sleeping
Next to each other on that spare bed
After our night out in Budapest

We said good morning
To the others,
>   in higher voices

Our faces contorted,
to control our emotions and noises

Our flushed cheeks, caught red-handed
to prevent the escape
>   of nervous laughter

And when they rolled back to sleep
We dove back under the covers
Our lips eager to meet
in teenage recklessness
>   — distorted teenage dream

Everything is so much more fun
When you're not meant to do it

sneaking out of the house
taking a cookie out of the jar
kissing him in secret
trying desperately to be quiet
so that no one else would be alerted – or throw a pillow at your
head
because it was too much of a display of
affection

or worse

because they would be awoken

Ha
[Laughs]
Remember when you were younger
And you actually had to plan
Of the safe places
Of where you could have sex
Without someone accidentally
Walking in

Ha
[Laughs]
How your problems change
Now as an adult
It's more like
Finding someone
You actually want to have sex with

                                    – how your problems change

we used to cross the forest
to go to the toilet
so we could steal more kisses together

what a childish affair
we brought blankets
to the wilderness
to mess around in the open air

Nature could watch us
Nature could judge us
Our secrets were out and bared

we were just two teenagers,
interested in exploring
each other's bodies,
as that was our whole world instead

— reckless

We were not fill in the blanks
We were limitless

    A blank page that we could do whatever with

        Create an epic novel
        Paint a masterpiece and pastel it autumn
        The colours bursting sunrise and dawn
        Our signatures sat side by side at the bottom
        The main value of the artefact

we.

we gave it importance

– co-signatories

***

i dreamt that music was colour and i could paint

There was lightning on the beach
But we didn't care
We danced on the sand
Our hands in the air
The rain ballooned and poured
The waves crashed in fours
The thunder erupted and roared

We?
We just kept spinning
And spinning
Then soared

– lightning glass

***

Gravity couldn't have stopped us
even if it tried
we were weightless
infinite
airborne in the sky

***

my favourite kinds of clouds are cumulonimbus clouds
they sound funny
and are fluffy like a hotel pillow
I like the idea that they start of as one thing
and then evolve into a
force to be reckoned with

***

every young girl needs to be single for a while
to learn how to love herself
and then to re-learn how to do so
again and again

– youthful discipline

***

she attuned
Like a musical note on a Yamaha piano
To fit into the surroundings around her

she forgot
That she is the main piece in an orchestra
And that silence can befall on the whole opera house
To hear her speak

– the grand piano

***

you will emerge like a flower
rising
from the concrete
surpassing
its limits
you weren't meant to
go against gravity
and yet you did

you grew against all the laws of life
you flower in the concrete

practice saying no in the mirror
like reps you do at the gym
three times a week
ideally, try to do it daily
as if popping pills or vitamin Cs down the back of your throat
daily affirmations to say no
pucker your cheeks
purse your lips
enunciate
state it clearly, the two letters
so even in situations you don't want to do, don't want to go,
don't want to be
it'll come out more easily
the small burst of air
with all the power wielded behind it

                                           – no.

———

another exercise:
apologising more,
with humility,
and accepting apologies,
with grace

– I forgive

hold people you love closely
you never know which moment is going to be the last

———

– remorse
I'm always thinking about her
I don't think I'm over the fact that
I couldn't save her
and couldn't help her
and was helpless

***

Is it just me, or has anyone else found face-to-face
break-ups really weird?
there's just this *one* precise moment
when the conversation becomes too convoluted
too many heated words exchanged
zig-zagged into a toddler's scribbles
and you think, oh shit
we can't go back
I can't forgive
it's gone past the point of no return
we will never again share a kiss

fuck, I'll never again
taste your lips

– the final moment

      try to never walk away from a fight
you won't always be able to apologise after

***

      if you could go back
      would you have run after them

                                                  yes

***

Felix

      when he rests his head on my lap
      I want his sorrow to leach into my skin
      the way spilled tea soaks into paper,
      with no control

but

    we were in a blue lagoon
submerged in our
promise of something new,

        sitting idly in
rock pools of ignorance
combing our hair
    when we heard the sirens from afar.

      they were approaching
  quick
with green tails thrashing
    and lullabies for voices that were

            screeching

When you say you got in a car crash
Everyone assumes you're somehow at fault
That you were reckless

No one ever assumes
You were innocent
Minding your own business
When the car slammed into your side dashboard
And the windows shattered out

– car crash

***

He yanked me under
Like a riptide
And made me drift so far out at sea
I could not see the shore anymore

———

It started off calm
And easy
I was drifting on my back
easing into the blue sky
Floating atop the calm sea
and then it happened.

    your love was so powerful,
    it struck me like a lightning bolt
    hurt like one too

        too bad I didn't listen,
        to my doubts and intuition
        too bad I ended up dead and
abused

he affected my ability to breathe
covered my screaming mouth
with both his hands
then lips
he was a psychopath

it was painful,
the way I had to leave

***

I blazed bright
And then plunged
A meteor from the sky

***

and the heavens split open
and poured
the lightning flashed
and roared
saturating the ground with its anger

***

[welcome to learning lesson 101]
on empathy and self-compassion

It is a well-known psychology trick to treat yourself
like you would, to a younger version of yourself
well what if you wanted to tell yourself
to <u>stop</u> wearing those hideous tights in 2009

―――――

I'm kidding
Sometimes I wish I could seize the younger me by the shoulders
And scream
GET THE HELL OUT
Don't go down this path
I know it looks like a decent plan now
But just TRUST ME
ABORT ABORT ABORT

―――――

do you hear that
what?
The screaming
from a small her

Other times, I wish I could tell the younger me
    With an exasperated sigh
    and closed eyes
    Ok, fine just do it
    But do it quick
    Just rip it off like a band-aid
    Or else it'll leave scars that you'll only piece together
when you're an adult
    And you're trying (and failing) to process them through
    With a counsellor

    They'll call it "growth" and "learning"
    So who knows?
    Maybe it is common,
        necessary,
    Even *good* – for the developmental process
    So sure, knock yourself out kiddo
    Fuck us up

---

    then when it's quiet
    and we're both subdued
    we'll sit next to each other
    legs extended out
    a comfort juice box in hand
    and when it happens
    her slow convulses, shoulders shuddering
    as she cries

I'll hold her
gentle because I'm not sure how to
but gentle nonetheless, as I'll go through the same
emotion twice

---

and when it ends
I'll wipe her tears
hand her a tissue to blow her nose
and wrap her in a big blanket

making sure it covers her toes so she stays warm
in a self-made burrito fort
and I'll tell her
I'm sorry we're hurting
        and that we continue to do so
just know
It's ok
You'll survive
even though it doesn't feel like it sometimes
you're stronger than you think
and the pain will fade
so much so that you'll even forget it
barely recall it when you stumble upon it, years later
find it and pull it out
from the corners of your heart
and you'll struggle to remember, to categorise what it is
it won't hurt anymore
you're safe

***

I'd stare at one of my professors sometimes
I wasn't fond of her
Not that there was anything wrong with her
It was just because she taught the subject I detested the most
(yes, I'm really that logical)

anyways, I'd stare at her and think
isn't it strange
disliking her when all she wants is happiness
like the rest of us.
like every single person I passed when taking the tube, to sit in this lecture hall among the sea of students,
    at the back, with a hoodie pulled up
(who am I kidding, I streamed this at home on the couch)
  we all just want
  happiness.
  no suffering.
      continually seeking pleasure through the senses

I'd sit there and think
(instead of paying attention to the liabilities incurred in tort law or whatever else)
why is this the case though?
    why do we all want,
      quick happiness
      and nothing else

***

so as good practice
Here's a list of painful human experiences:

wet socks
when there's a discount on your favourite expensive ice cream brand and the flavour you want is all out
just missing your bus even though you tried running for it
missing the last train
missing anything really –
your person
because it's the wrong place, wrong time
try the next life pal
(though chances are, you'll miss each other again)

your alarm in the morning
when you take a nap but you wake up even more tired than before you slept
when your hair tie snaps
when it's the middle of winter and you can't find your lip balm and your lips are really chapped
(don't lick your lips, that just makes it worse)

when you lose one earring so they don't match
paper cuts
the death of a loved one
heartbreak

death tax

like why even – which deranged sadistic government official thought it would be a good idea to slap people with taxes and bureaucracy, when they're in the middle of grieving

when it rains and your umbrella breaks
or
having to walk alone after a breakup, in the pouring rain, with your grocery bags (and some Doritos) and no umbrella (because did you not read? you have no hands, since you're carrying groceries)
looking like a drenched cat
sleeping with someone whom you thought was an 8, but when morning came, they were more of a 4

not having the last coin when you have all the others to make up for the 95 cents to pay for your iced tea at the local convenience store

spilling food on your favourite top
spilling wine –
anywhere
because you've just wasted wine

your ex moving on and looking happier
their new person more interesting and attractive than you
lipstick on your teeth

food stuck in your teeth (and when it's really obvious like kale)

and worst of all, you were just trying to chat up the cute person next to you

sitting on your glasses and hearing them break

failed attempts to look dignified

blinking in a group photo

and you can't delete it because it was taken on someone *else's* phone

when you thought you were cool enough to cut your own hair

what your parents dressed you in when you were younger

your glasses fogging up when entering a room or eating udon

when you open the fridge and you realise your flatmates ate your takeaway food that you were saving (and you don't know which flatmate)

when you're about to have sex with a stranger and you realise there's no more condoms left

(fuck)

world poverty

malaria

cancer

writing your CV

job interviews

smiling during job interviews
oh what are my strongest qualities?
why, it's

no more toilet paper...when you're on the toilet
nude picture leaks
misogyny
crazy stalkers
being a woman

herpes

when you wear sexy lingerie just for them to take it right off
period cramps
being over/underdressed when everyone else isn't
your vibrator running out of battery
people claiming the earth is flat

mosquito bites
mosquito bites on your face making it look like a pimple
school picture day
getting hit in the face with a volleyball
waving to someone who you thought was waving to you but wasn't
being forced to talk to your relatives on the phone
human trafficking
learning a new language
logarithms

    just math in general
    being right on the cusp of cumming and then not because they stopped that exact motion
    idiots

traffic
missing your flight because of traffic
because you forgot your passport
because of delays
because of *you know*, "unforeseen weather circumstances"
really, shitty people
your co-workers
your ex-boyfriend

smug successful people
with nice soap in their bathrooms and holiday greeting cards
haemorrhoids
social media influencers
with too many ads
vomiting
and diarrhoea
vomiting whilst having diarrhoea
(more is not necessarily better)
    working out every day for a fortnight to only gain more weight (when that wasn't your intention)

    a good moment not being able to last

when it's too cold outside and then too hot on the subway, it's rush hour and your face is in someone else's armpit and you can barely breathe

    not being taller

    smelly teenage boys underwear

    puberty

    zits in awkward places like elbows or your left butt cheek

    dentists

    accidentally biting your tongue when chewing

    war and genocide

    mould on your food products or belongings

    because humidity

    seeing very little in your bank account

    student debt

    suicide

    getting left behind

    stubbing your toe

    really stupid people

    and being stuck in a conversation with them

    posh people who aren't actually posh

    being single when you want to be in a relationship

    being in a relationship when you want to be single

    because your partner is a twit

    or it started of good and then the honeymoon period passed

    and you realise you're just totally not compatible together and it should end quickly

domestic violence

cheaters

stumbling on your words when you're trying to make a point

losing a fight

crying when you're losing a fight

slamming the door behind you and it didn't slam

liars

the ones who said they "didn't study" but then did

or claimed they "also did really bad on the exam" and got an A –

ugly accents

poor tippers

disagreeable pins and needles

when you really need to pee

lost packages

delayed packages

bombs

Karens

bad singing by people who think they're really good

wanting to sleep but having too many thoughts and not being able to –

or worse, when you can't and you're fully conscious that you need to wake up early the next day – tick tock tick tock –

dress codes

not being able to illegally stream movies
slow internet

bad report cards
popcorn that didn't fully pop
no sweet option at the cinema
no regular coke, just diet
blowing up a balloon and it bursts

Christmas crackers with no present inside
towels that aren't even fully dry
your phone running out of battery with no charger in sight
overpopulation
male dictators
being cute on the beach interrupted by attacking sandflies
getting a period stain
on anything (both at home and in public)
a flat tyre
the snow melting before you get to play in it
sitting at home during the New Year countdown to watch the fireworks on TV
or worse,
sleeping through it

global warming killing the reefs
and when you go scuba diving, all the coral is bleached and it's really quite selfish, because now you can't have any pretty pictures to show off to your friends

eye infections
gonorrhoea
running out of bus money
having a runny nose and no tissues
going on holiday for it to rain for the week
long lines at the amusement park
someone stealing your parking space after a ten-minute wait
road rage

finding out that you weren't invited to the group gathering
that your best friend replaced you
losing friends in general
losing stuff
at home, outside, in the restaurant, in the cab
misplacing your dignity
politicians
a noisy toddler on an eight-hour flight
a kicker behind you on a red eye
turbulence
being grounded
weak water pressure in the shower
dumb people wasting water
water scarcity
the household using up all the hot water after the Boxing Day walk

your earphones after digging them up from your pocket
(they are. always. tangled.)

being lousy at sports
uncoordinated in general
Bambi on ice (goodbye magical moments at Somerset House)
unreasonable rules and regulations
chores
listening to the stories of peoples' gap years
an ugly tan
a really nice day at the beach but it's too crowded
you get in the water and then get sunburnt
stung by a jellyfish

slapping a stranger's ass in the grocery store because you thought it was your sibling's
being slapped in the face
exams
when you mess up your signature and someone was watching
bad dreams and nightmares
seeing someone eat a booger.

grapes with seeds that were so-called "seedless"
nails scratching on a chalkboard
saying goodbye to your pet
slipping on a wet patch
urgently needing the bathroom and there are none available
or if you're simply female –
because there's always a really long queue outside the ladies

(can someone please explain to me how this phenomenon occurs on a <u>global</u> scale)
    receiving bad news
    not getting laid

    traveling alone so you can't sleep
    because you'll miss your transit
    or someone can easily steal your bags
    actually having your belongings stolen
    when there are no subtitles to the foreign film you wanted to watch
    when your sports team didn't win
    when your idol marries someone else

    when there's no salt or ketchup or vinegar for your fries
    just barbecue sauce
    when you open a 'bag' of crisps
    full stop.
    or when the crisps are broken and sad
    when the cookie snapped when you dipped it in milk
    eating too much at a buffet cause you're cheap and now you're paying the price – cause you're stuck in the toilet – doubled over in pain – you're straining so much – there's tears in your eyes –
    finally, after what feels like an hour – coming out to wash your hands and the person next to you didn't
    or everyone heard you and are averting their eyes
    you watch someone apply lipstick and then witnessed a murder, as they jammed the lid back on and squished the colour

when you. absolutely. annihilate your comb
cause your hair is so tangled, you can't untangle it
when your sibling tattletaled on you
or successfully framed you for something you didn't do –
jet lag
migraines and toothaches
when you go to a concert, cinema, theatre and there's a really tall person in front of you

when someone skips the queue
and you're too shy to say anything
dropping an egg on the floor
and needing to clean it up
when the fizzy drink is no longer fizzy
or when the food is not spicy enough
your dog loving your parents more than you
the food only lukewarm, not piping hot
a broken phone screen
a break up text
that you read with a broken screen
realising you've been blocked
watching others be promoted
rejection
being given a small scoop of ice cream by the ice cream guy – which at first you were hesitant, since it was expensive to buy – but you then swallowed the painful cost in the name of self-love – well that backfired spectacularly well – and *then* a bad thought arose – was it because they didn't find you pretty enough?

motion sickness

all your friends being hit on

but you on a night out

falling for a prank

being stuck in a group project with a really lazy member (what an inconsiderate nonce)

your sibling finding the love of their life and not confiding in you anymore

babysitting screaming children (*any* child; related or not)

giving birth

failing your driving test because you messed up parallel parking

needing to contact customer service

ironing

shitty presents and pretending to like them

a banging outfit but it's not in your size

growing old

hangovers

growing old and not being able to deal with hangovers well anymore

bullies

entry level jobs but "with 5 years minimum work experience" (I see you the UN)

sticky keyboards

the air-con being broken on a summer day

when you have to work overtime

cracking an egg and oh look, there's broken eggshell inside –
leg day
bad hair day
when you run out of mascara
when it smudges
uneven eyeliner, even though you already applied it three times
insecurity
finding out that Santa isn't real

when you didn't click record
or save
your laptop crashes
a hole in your pocket
when you were so looking forward to having sex but you're severely bloated

when they tell you they don't love you any longer

alright, now let's try this with good experiences
jk

we somehow gain happiness when talking about our sufferings

***

you sadistic fuck

i like walking around in cemeteries
and contemplating death
or hunting for deer at Richmond Park
feasting my eyes on wilderness
the way they roam

***

[brake]

Have you ever seen a deer in headlights?
That's me
when a stranger asks:
"Where do you come from?"
I balk.

an innocent question, so many intonations

do you want the long or the short answer?
passport or emotion?
it also depends who's asking:
do they look like me?
are they trying to figure out my accent? nationalistic, xenophobic
do they actually care?
when they talk, do they talk in cursive?
around bushes and roundabouts
what is their purpose
intention?
deep breath,

it's complicated
I was born here, but moved around a lot

now I sound like an asshole
and now you've got me doubting myself

***

I have a deep unseated desire to please
    authority
    anyone
always hoping
do you like me?

***

my throat was grated sandpaper
I was a dying man
Under the weight of the desert
With no love

— parched

***

I pressed the
pockets and valves of my heart
like flower petals
in between the pages of an encyclopedia
gentle but firm
with the intention
of preserving her longer

                                          — encyclopedia

***

I have been conditioned
culturally
to obey
others would call it submission
    it works for the economy
    docile, pliant workers
    it works for the country
    yielding, manageable citizens
yes I am a people-pleaser but remember
I
bear down the weight of centuries-old traditions
and dynasties that have thrived and failed because of this
without question
filial piety
reverence
the need to put others before you
and your own comfort

it is hard struggling with what is expected
and what you want
when those needs directly conflict one another

it is hard looking back on choices and decisions
on moments when you wish you could have stood up for yourself
and been more assured
to do what is right

against authority
even when they are your own bosses or elders

it is not easy when your two sides
diametrically oppose

what you have been brought up with since birth
influenced by your parents, your family and society
with what you have seen and experienced
in your travels and growth

which side is correct
if at all
is it right
to neglect others who have more life experience
is it wise
to act on emotion,
when it can be fleeting and short-term
is it better
to bite your tongue but know you'll survive
        courage is good
        preserving oneself is good
        but should it be tempered

                I was just trying to be agreeable

      don't ask me for advice

***

communicating with immigrant parents
is difficult sometimes:
the language barriers
cultural differences
generational gap

the issue is that our love
is expressed in different ways
we have different needs
and can't communicate

I could feel my cry
stuck in my chest
like a piece of food lodged in my throat
I couldn't breathe
I couldn't breathe
I couldn't speak
I couldn't speak
our kitchen table wasn't wide
but it felt like we were sitting across oceans
              in different continents, sometimes

I'm a lot more eloquent when I write
compared to when I speak
Maybe the whole world
maybe we could just write love letters to each other

***

let me haul up the dredges
sift through the sand
pull up my memories
from my brain to my hands

— crumbling sandcastles

***

inhale the sand of a desert
the dust in the air
the headiness of a crowd
their sweat, shouts and shoves
of leather from their bags
the squeal of trolley brakes
savour their language
how it rolls from their tongue

breathe in the frankincense

— the Middle East

there'll be this place
that you'll get to grow up in when you're older
where the mountains frame your sight
where the buildings are all white, beige or cream
and the roofs are flat
where it stills your heart
and quietens it with peace
where life is simple
and this simplicity resounds in the sand
where the sun burns
against the bright blue
and some days will bless you
with orange sunset skies
so intense
it is only fit for a painter
such as Rothko
          Picasso
                    or Matisse
the reds and pinks so vivid
like Bougainvilleas
it would make them drool
    and fling themselves to the ground
in a desperate attempt
to capture it onto the easel

it would not be for Sisley

who desires genteel

or softness

curdled lime greens and soft blue sea-foam

no no

this is

the eruption

of light

– Oman

***

different types of loving
is like smoking
culturally acceptable in some places
more open and
exuberant in those places

for others to only smoke in private
after sex
like an exhale of
private thoughts for oneself
but nonetheless,
       it is the breathing in
of something foreign into one's own system
and making it theirs

                                         – cigarettes

***

[my mix tape] gramophone records

dim the lights
drop the needle down
sit there on your couch
head back
breathe
strap in for the ride
of emotions and
nostalgia

———

your first crush
— when you're young and you don't even talk to them but it still gives you butterflies

He rode his bike to school
beside my car
He'd chase me down
to see who would get there first

It was an unspoken promise between us
to reach school early
So we could share a private moment
between the two of us

a smile
before the front door would open and
Our classmates would come spilling in

and the spell would be broken
till the next day

---

young romance

It's quiet and it's dark
Two hands clutching the phone receiver
"I like you," you breathe with bated breath
"I like you too," they reply back
Relief floods your chest
after months of going back and forth
shy conversations leading nowhere
quick glances and small smiles reserved just for you –
it happened
You feel like crying from happiness
life is sweet and merry and bright and
the world is yours to bask in

    Relive in
    The first times
    The foolish promises
    The fights and arguments
    And awkward conversations
        This is your first relationship

———

        We bounded into a new promise
          Of something unknown
        Our steps wide and awkward
   – and yet
        floating
                and buoyant –
      the first team on the moon

———

    my first love
    I got butterflies
even when our hands were just side by side, barely touching
    both painfully and vividly aware
    that we could reach out and touch each other

    we used to hold hands underneath the table
not because we were doing it in secret, but because we were young
    and shy and felt like it would burst from our chest

                      – butterflies

***

let me levitate
and be deliriously happy

I say that but in hindsight
        it is better to wish for contentment than
                happiness,
  which is fleeting

      – there's a big difference between theory and practical

***

Man, you go through so many highs and lows in a single day
A rollercoaster of emotion
But without the fun

It's exhausting really
He loves me
He loves me not
We're together
Now we're swat

                        – rollercoaster

it's heaven and hell
but we're walking on earth

***

the way we cling onto one another
and wrap up so tightly
we are
vines strangling
each other

***

you'd read to me
with your arms around me
to let me drift off into sleep
our friends would come in
and disturb us and make fun of you
but you didn't care
it was sweet but was it really
was it because you wanted points
to tick off milestones
I really don't know
or was it because you liked how it felt
seeing me smile
my shyness peering out from behind the curtained stairwell
or was it for you
to keep someone warm and to
prevent yourself from being alone

[cause it's easier and more fun to row a boat in pairs
than on your own,
where you have to chart your way
and steer whilst paddling,
a little too much for a single multi-tasking]

so
I guess we're back to the start now
it's back to you
and your reading voice
speak louder my dear, it's hard to hear you above ~~myself,~~
the noise

— bedtime milestones

---

it's hard growing up
being unsure of thoughts and insecurity
and how to weed them out from sincerity

— the best backhands are often delivered on your own

***

He's a good soldier
He takes any job seriously
to the point of physical collapse
I wonder if he loves me
because he believes that it is his stoic duty
a post he cannot give up

Or whether it's cause he would do so anyways
even if it was forbidden
to the point that he would face the firing squad
with love bared on his chest
in brave declaration

— an attempt at love, with questionable intentions

———

                did you latch on tight
                after i told you 'i love you'
                because i precisely told you that

***

he wore a necklace
and used to lend it to me
we'd sit on the bleachers holding hands
not talking much
he wasn't much of a talker
I didn't know anything about him
not truly
of what was inside his head
of what was happening at home
we just sat and talked about us and our future

it was careless really

―――――

we couldn't separate love from lover,
couldn't separate fact from sin

I was too self-assured
You were the opposite
   so self-conscious

      your cat is still the only cat that has ever liked me
it's embarrassing really

[a letter]

I see why you listened to metal music
as a teen
I just wanna empty my lungs
and scream

***

do you remember the first night we spent together
how it was a bit messy
a bit awkward
limbs everywhere
almost thrashing
teeth clashing
shoulders banging

we were ripe with beginning
it was too ripe
almost rotting

– rotting

I think he knows
that you're not as into him
as he is into you

***

I used him as support crutches
but I knew I had to let him free

it was hard
we were comfortable, had instinctive trust and faith

but there were bouts of feelings
I wanted to fly
someone to match my dreams

***

for
watching the tops of clouds
on a plane
is a whole other feeling
why it makes you feel pristine

for
you spend most of your life on the ground
and suddenly you're cruising at high heights
gazing
beneath

— tops of clouds

---

one of the nicest feelings
is having the window seat on a plane
and watching it touchdown
into your hometown at night
with the blinking lights and winking sights
of blue and gold
welcoming you home

there's so much light pollution in cities
that even when the lights are out
and it's night,
it still looks like twilight

———

prop the window slightly ajar —
let it in
to soak it in
the blare of the ambulance
its sirens wailing in the distance
the laughter of drunkards &
uni students stumbling back from a night out
after a cheeky pitstop
        at the fast food joint
feel the pierce of the winter chill
above the radiator's heat
smell your neighbour's garbage
because they didn't tie it properly
and a fox mauled into it
let the city flood your senses
before you get some sleep

                    — outlandish noise [cause cities can't sleep]

———

      it's never quiet in cities
           somebody's always up and miserable

***

Whose bright idea was it
To flood the subway with harsh white light
      No one looks good under it
        No one.
      The tiredness more pronounced
Scars and pockmarks permanently etched
      Eyes haggard
      The blackheads on your nose like
      The textured skin of a strawberry
      It's unflattering
      To be awash with sterile light
      How can anyone fall in love with me organically on
the way to work

                – under fluorescence

after the pandemic

I savoured

sitting close to people

on the train

the slight touch of clothes brushing upon each other

Someone's sneakers next to mine

human contact –

really,

I missed it

as if

I had been starving and parched for all this while

I needed it

as

I felt empty inside

in other words

not myself

                                        lost

afterwards

just no
no no no no no
I don't want to hear it
or see it
the letters
even strung up on a golden necklace
spelling
p a n d e m i c
no more
maybe I can block it out – ~~the whole experience~~ – like how I blot the oil on my nose
with blotting paper when I'm in southeast Asia

Singapore

I took it for granted
how things just work
and are convenient
and modern
and clean
in our city

I failed to fully appreciate
the lack of dust
when fingers traced, the moving train
in light touch

how the pavements are so pristine
it looks washed and clean, almost antiseptic
you would dare to lick it

and how the arms of rain trees
stretched to the sky
the roads wide enough for a plane to land
in planned execution
how things are so convenient, its medical system

you forget
that you can trust and depend on a system
    if you called help
    you would receive it

leave your laptop in the coffee shop
when you go to the dentist
no double take
    glance back
    hesitation

good Samaritans
variety of food selection
with reasonable prices
prices that don't slaughter you or make you think
is this the way things should be

open air hawkers
clean line towers
the juxtaposition, a thought theory desired
harmonic utopia
    you judge
    but what do you do better
at least it attempts
to put it in practice
to prioritise its citizens

it's not perfect
but which country is
it had a big dream
and tried to achieve it
it's small
but stood firm in chaos   with reason

it learnt from others
and made things its own
it stayed focused
with its eyes beyond the Straits of Malacca
                                      the horizon
it did better than simply
staying afloat

———

it's not easy
keeping up the juggling pins all at once
in aired suspension
whilst trying to remain true
to yourself
and paving your own way,
in the circus
of global diplomacy
after a peacetime of eight decades

it's like the jungle of high school
but in real life
expanded to a global magnitude

a circus act

she sits
like an orchid
on display in the hotel lobby

elegant
and serene

they forget
she thrives in the wilderness, on trees
untamed and epiphytic
on top of vines
in the tropics

– orchid flower

I am most proud of the
integrity
and the
trust in our system
the minimisation of
    corruption

        for
        I have seen
            too many
        nations

        and its people
bleed
        because of their leaders
        and their movement

the after-wave shocks
and ripples
from the epicentre

        the cleanup
        that takes years
        it's almost impossible

but I am a perfectionist
I am scared of speaking up
but even more scared of staying silent

we are a country
of contrasts
and opposites

        rectangles
        straight lines
        containers
        nestled in greens

cultures
traditions
history
overtaken by modern gleams
nature is wrestled
into organised boxes
the phrase – [garden city]
is what people know us as

      I want to be more
           I want to be better
      I want to be more than an airport
      where people only pause
      to transit
      and never linger
                      – Changi

———

its construct
to confront
in full pulse

———

      i sometimes wonder
      whether the laws that are set down in stone
      are they there to protect us
      or to prevent us
                 – the bedrock of society

———

       the age-old question
       moral quandary
            & dilemma
       head-scratcher, uncracked riddle
       on loop insomnia

       which came first
       the chicken or the egg?

       rules
       cameras
       big brother

       or

       safety
       harmony
       silence

       i'm perplexed

                                            – riddle

———

they lend credence
to my thoughts and questions
but you don't
i feel you want me stunted

———

you teach me how to
read well
& complete the sums
& regurgitate the facts
but you don't teach me how to
think for myself

———

i know you go to the other room
to talk about me
in hushed voices, low tones, strained murmurs
i don't know how i feel about it though
i suppose i should be honoured

i know you care for me
but i wish you would understand –
that sometimes
all i need is a hug
and a held eye gaze
look deep into my inner world
touch me and my vulnerable soul
to tell me, i hear you
i understand, i'm listening

that would be better than this.
this is stifling

– an adult conversation

growing up means a lot of alone time
with your own thoughts

– I hear them loud and clear

***

[people-watching]
it's great catching the bus to the airport in the dead of night at 4am. in doing so, you share the bus with other tightfisted travellers like yourself, party animals, immigrants and hard-working single parents, coked up corporate addicts dabbled in power/powder/money or all three. the last group is a lie. they would never use public transport.   in your best attempt to not fall asleep, you can people-watch [the aforementioned list], make up stories in your head, as the bus rumbles to different parts of the city to pick up more weary travellers.

and yet, despite this, despite the crowd and the people at any point in time, day or night, one can feel so inexplicably lonely

– in a big city

***

if one is a country boy
you'll adore cities
the people, the energy, the buzz
how sometimes, you can scarcely hear your own thoughts
how you're assaulted by every car and picture in front of your eyes
indeed. you'll relish every moment that your lungs can barely
expand under the soot, smog and aromatics of kebab stalls,
vinegar-doused chippies and burnt aftershave from barber shops
yeah, most of you guys love the cities

fuck oxygen and the need to breathe
one thing cities have that are plentiful
young people
potential mating partners and fuck buddies

                                                    – country boy in a city

***

narrow paths and swollen gutters
winding streets no hidden cover
gloomy lamps where figures huddle
underneath
      & the dark puddles streeeetch
            in a pool of blood –
trudge along

with your hood over your ears
your hands deep in your pockets

baby grow up

peel the gum from your shoe
and avert your eyes from the guy
taking a piss facing the road
on a Sunday morning

don't pay for the bus fare
when you only ride two stops
the trick is to sneak around the back when someone else is exiting
two ships passing in the dead of night – with the stealth of a
morning fog that appeared and vanished as suddenly as it came –
duck
hide behind the lady's jacket then nip up the stairs
sit in your seat
quick
look out the window
pretend that you've been there all this time

ah cities,
the opportunities are endless
morality is senseless

what a fucking riot
                it is

***

when you live in a city
there is always someone out there
hurting because of a broken heart
as well as someone
having sex

— hard truths

***

seriously, that is my thought process when I'm suffering from a broken heart.
    [my stupid heart, why won't you learn]
I'd try to tell myself – your experience is no different from any other. there's literally millions of us wounded here, dying from this heartbreak. we're all laying crumpled, on the bedroom floor, worn out from crying – I'd repeat this to myself as I'm laying there, trying to talk myself out of the hurt, surrounded by used tissues dotted like large, stupid daisies in the grass, waiting, but hardly patient, just restless for the skies to change colour – and I'd try to imagine invisible strings floating out from the window, connecting me with all the other broken beings in the rest of the cityscape.
    in the midst of my misery

— invisible strings

oh cities

how wonderful you are

how i can cry out loud in the middle of your belly

and not pretty cry

but *bawl*

loud, ugly sounds

with fat, ugly tears

and it's perfectly fine

it just happens

the cars roll by

the traffic continues and people walk on and don't look back

these are normal tidings

these are stomach rumblings

it's normal, you tell me, after a dinner course

everyone goes through indigestion

aka. heart ache

– angina

If you're sad but functioning
you're doing well
give yourself a star
sticker

cause you're trying to mend yourself and
pray that the damage doesn't develop
into a keloid scar
god I'm bitter

———

I'm sorry I wrote to you
It was a moment of desperation
A plea
I didn't mean to
Not truly
Well kinda
Sincerely
I just wanted to speak to somebody
Someone who knew me and
Someone who used to want me

– desperate

  it takes time to nurse your wounds.
a lot of time, because the injuries can erupt in all sorts of forms:
1) lacerations, 2) punctures, 3) abrasions, 4) grazes, 5) contusions
1) the timing is off, 2) betrayal, 3) growing apart, 4) too many
fights till it hits the breaking point,
5) falling out of love with one another

   lesions suck
   don't do long distance

             – lifeguarding love lessons

I drew a wide berth
From the boy with the disarming smile

          too bad I am lousy in maths
      and couldn't use a protractor for my life
           I mistook obtuse for acute
            so the bad boys ran rife

 – numeracy skills

***

you are
inexorably
treacherous

when we met again
you acted
like
you had amnesia about our history
you dick
did it only matter to me –

and after I put in all this effort to look extra hot tonight
I wanted to watch you squirm
and burn
in discomfort
with longing
and apologies
to beg me to take you back

I wanted to be surrounded by people
in a thousand laughs
to have the perfect lighting on me
shining me aglow
my brilliance so bright that
you had to squint
when you caught sight of me from across the room

I wouldn't be the one to approach you.
you would
saying, "hey, you look good"
"you know what? I'm so sorry, words don't even cut it"
to which I could look you in the eye
and say
"I'm happier now"
"It's water under the bridge now"
to hopefully have the mental willpower
to tell you no.
"I'm good thanks"
before sashaying away
to engage in another conversation
in a throng of friends, still utterly radiant
after which the hottest person in the room
would descend upon me in that instant
and shower me with copious amounts of attention

and you'd be open-mouthed
flabbergasted
like a goldfish
at a loss of words
dumbfounded
basically an abyss

you'd see me painted in a halo
cascaded in heavenly light
laughing, with a large flourish of my smile

my fingers elegant and outstretched
my hair like a shampoo ad windswept
the hot dude leaning in closer to me as we speak,
it appears as if we're engaged in a steamy kiss –
your panic is bubbling
you're finding it hard to resist – from screaming NOOO –
you want to march over and yank us apart
but your legs are lead and they're parked
your mind just whizzing, a complete blur
just like your very worst nightmare rolled in a curse
your brain in full speed all questions no answers
your emotions zigzagging like cancerous dancers
        where did it go wrong,
        what did *you* do wrong,
you're in full throttle – the mode *reminisce* –
        the highlight reel before you watch
           your own figure torch it
                with gasoline

...

    instead

    we're both sat separately
    in our separate conversations
    our eyes have not met each other's
    you have not approached me

        you have moved on
        you're not even testing the waters
        or even glancing over

it's pathetic really
me pining for you
and acting like I don't care

      – and the Oscar award goes to "x"

---

you should always dress up
with the assumption that you will bump into your ex

---

      i hate you, you suck
      go shit yourself, you fuck
      you broke my heart
      snapped it apart
trod on it for good measure and spat on it for luck

      – how things flipped, a limerick

                    my lonely heart cried out
                       can someone hear me
                        can someone listen
                                  anyone

                  can you fall in love with me
                                and find me
                                  endlessly
                                interesting

---

when hot water
feels like a lover's embrace

and you stand in the shower for so long
the heat runs out

---

maybe I should buy a weighted blanket
to relieve my stress
and the weight
of feeling
alone

and it was around noon
when I realised this afternoon
with a *jolt*
that the first word I think of
when I see the letter 'L'
is loser
and not love

— loser, not love

---

you left indentations
in my skin
like my ring
after wearing it too long in the shower
or to sleep for weeks

you changed my body physically
left marks
as if to *highlight* and <u>underline</u> my alteration,
like the orange designs left from henna

I noticed these changes
with a pang –
some pain
because you were no longer there
some shame
because you changed me
before leaving

— indentations

and
>   exhaaaaale

[pause]

breathe out the years of memories
and history
of inside jokes and hidden stories
the fingerprints he left all over your heart
and hands

breathe out the fact that he just told you
he's into someone else

breathe out the loving

[what really stings] + any synonym of *hurts*

when you see how they treat the one after you
the one they properly like.
and you think
ah
that's how you should have treated me
that's how things should have been
>   between us

that's how things wouldn't have ended,
if you had liked me that way
if you had liked me enough

it's a pity it took years

———

I like her
he says
of course you do
he didn't have any money to spend on
you
to go on trips with you
(he was saving – you understood – he had a part-time job
to fund for school)
but of course he did for her
of course it was before he was actually earning
                                      was there any excuse?
        not really

it was a small getaway
borrowed his Mum's Mazda for a couple days
booked a bed and breakfast in a quaint cottage
                       for the two of them
they went to the outskirts

                                    – it was a small getaway

she's away now
    but we're trying to plan for her to come back soon

he couldn't do long distance for you
but of course
he ~~could~~ can for her

———

        swallow that ashen taste in your mouth
          sit with the heaviness in your heart
            then hear that voice in your bones
      you should have been treated better all that while
                    my dear

———

to make a commitment to someone
and then to watch it fall apart
is a
very very
peculiar feeling indeed
it's like the world's emotions in one

Do you think they were always like this throughout the whole relationship?
That quiet bit of being selfish
Unwilling
  Whilst you gave your whole being?

***

she looked watered down
like the trails of ink disappearing down the sink
when washing the palette

– ink trails

***

I shed more layers when I go to my room
My bra
My dress
The smile on my face

It's like a chrysalis
Except backwards

– a butterfly death

ah, when you're downtrodden and downcast
don't go online
I repeat
don't look at your social media when you're feeling shit
with your life

———

                                      [you're watching on the sidelines]
                                                                  shunned aside
              the incompetent one on the bench during playoffs
                            whilst they go and live their life

———

how are you?
prone to loneliness

———

I look at babies and infants sometimes
and envy them
I'm jealous
of how they can scream and cry
and despite it all, they'll have someone at the end of the day
who will pick them up and soothe them

you think I'm joking

I'm really not

I wish it was appropriate

At age 24

To have a full on tantrum

Like a toddler flailing his arms

wanting sweets on aisle three

For it to be acceptable

And sometimes even

welcomed

Let it out

They would say

Gathering you in their arms

and swaddling you with gentle care and words

It's ok

I hear you

You're safe

I understand

They would rock you to sleep

and even buy the bag of sour candy you were holding

In your tightly clenched fist

So that you can have some later

when you feel better

and lighter

when you're all cried out

most of the time
i feel like
a Pollock painting

———

this is an issue
for I yearn to be
Monet's lilies

winter came
and froze her into icicles
she was beautiful
but cold
if she fell
she could pierce through your neck
whole

– icicles

***

I reached out for your hand
Without thinking
Turned around to tell you the funny story from today
instinctively

It's like the phantom feeling
soldiers get when their arms or limbs are missing
The feeling of what was once theirs, and what was once so natural
To flex their fingers when reaching for a glass of water,
or to outstretch their hand when opening a door handle,

that urge that still lingers and remains as second nature

Though now you're absent

– the phantom feeling

looking back
we were retrograde music
it sounds nice but it's a
        backwards melody
a mock summer
before the real thing
        a wet spring underneath the boughs
of Regent's park

the lead up to the main act,
a joker to the king

– mock summer

***

I sincerely hope you will never feel betrayed
    It's potentially worse than heartbreak

***

For sometimes, your heart breaks because things don't work out. You were too young, too immature, or too old, too serious. Sometimes it breaks for the most wholesome of reasons and for the *right* reasons and you smile through your tears because you have lived and you have learned and oh god, it *hurts*, but you know you will survive and the sun will once more shine and cast light over Brooklyn's bricks and fire escapes. Eventually.

    But betrayal?

    There is nothing quite like it.

***

You were too young
Too young,
Like a bud that had not yet opened

I was foolish
For loving you,
your potential
You weren't ready for the next step
Weren't ready to find a new place together
when we had already lived together for several years
It was the ultimate betrayal
You were my home
Then you weren't
You removed yourself from the equation
It was like facing a stranger,
someone unknown

You wanna know what it feels like?
It was like someone had yanked
The floor underneath me
And I was midair
– suspended for just a split second –
your vacant expression
before falling
falling
tumbling

and
then the impact
the full body crush

...

that's how it felt like
now you know
you said loyalty was your strongest suit
but it seems that traitor,
is better tailored to you

...

what saddens me is
you had free rein
in my abode,

you used to roam
freely
in my home

— your potential

the worst part is
you didn't betray me because
you wanted to double-cross
you essentially deserted
without a collaborator
cause you were too young, just too young
to properly know how to
serve a queen

in this realm,
you became the informer yourself

I could see it
written all over your face
it was the words you uttered
your single action, which gave your disloyalty away

you faltered
for a split second
and that second was too much

we built our empire together
it was equal, we said
then you turned around
and became uncomfortable of my sacrifice instead

you said
you didn't feel okay
pursuing this together
leading our rule
you didn't want to continue, forging our build
so you gave it up
and threw it away
poured it down the gutters and watched our efforts
swirl
like dregs
down the drain
but don't you know?
that leaders always have to sacrifice
to pursue their dream, their home

all Kings are unsettled
Louis without Versailles
The Greeks without their temples
even Pharaohs need a final resting place
to lie their heads
in their pyramids

you stabbed me
23 times
I was defenceless
when I asked you
you too, child?
then you fled the portico
and fled from my life

– Julius Caesar in the Theatre of Pompey

the irony is
you misled the two of us
didn't even think
didn't use your brain
you didn't just betray me.
you betrayed yourself.
you should have seen your face when you realised.
all your walls came crumbling down

---

your complexion
was ashen
like you had just seen the ghost
of my body you just murdered
you gasped
as you let go of the knife
from your hands

it clattered
in the halls
on the stone floor of our palace
my blood was pooling
already staining
fusing with the tapestry carpet
the embroidered one we picked out together

Help!
You cried
Your voice barely a whisper
Help! GUARDS! Louder, in horror

You killed me
with your betrayal
Held me in your arms as you realised
I was limp and lifeless
Betrayed by my closest confidant
my most trusted advisor
my protector of the night

As it dawned upon you
The terror in your eyes
widened
And stretched till your irises could no longer be seen.
your colour blocked out
from
your deadly sin

You did it yourself
from your own foolishness
without Macbeth's wife.
You killed Duncan
unfortunate,
without thinking twice.

And the tears poured down your face
from your eyes
you were inconsolable
you couldn't even deny

your unforgivable action
which you neither plotted nor contrived
you didn't mean to
just didn't understand
the gravity of the situation
resulted by your bloodied hands
you could only cry, contrite
beat your chest and
despise

you garbled
I'm sorry I'm sorry
grief-stricken and wretched
grabbed my collar
and buried your face in my chest
you were beside yourself
cause you knew
that certain actions cannot be reversed
once they're brought to light, in full view

but if seen by another,
one could argue or surmise
the rocking

                    the lamentation
              were almost as if you were
        attempting to self-soothe and pacify,

                it was to protect yourself, wasn't it?
                            a self-preservation
                                    device

                                    then
            the sound of footsteps clamouring and
                            steel banging
                                    came
                        you had no choice
                        but to be taken away
                        I'll give you that
                at least you took it in your stride
                        I felt rather sorry for you
                                    as
                        you were somewhat
                                innocent
                        it's not like you
                                calculated,
                            with deliberate
                        intention to beguile

            but for one who never wanted to be forgotten
                    for one who wanted a legacy
                                you led us

                                to our demise
                        our kingdom fell after that
                       and was wiped from the books
                            so quickly and precise

                                but then again
                                what did I know
                            I was lying on the floor
                          with the gaping flesh wound

                                what did I know
                         I was still looking out for you
                                in my ghost form

---

despite it all
despite everything
I could never bear to see you
distraught

in truth,
I wanted to comfort you
in my arms

as you crying was
something I always found
so devastating

I suppose all kingdoms still need

sewage systems

ours just flooded

with waste

to our necks

the bloated bodies of murdered corpses

floating atop

like fish

poisoned in the waters

of their own home

I'm living elsewhere now
But I still feel the damp of you
In my lungs

***

   You used to say sometimes – you were scared that I was never really there
    That it was too good to be true
      That we'd be walking in a grocery store and I'd disappear into
        another aisle

And you'd get a lurching feeling in your stomach
    As if I had never existed
      And it was all a dream that you fabricated

        funny

Cause you then ended things
like it was nobody's business

        – disappearance on aisle 3

      i'm suddenly standing outside
      with my bags around my ankles
      the crowd milling by
      the door slammed in my face

———

i no longer had keys in my pocket
        was chucked back – and stranded
on the streets' wide-open
            gaping mouth,
    homeless once more

it wasn't raining
    but it felt like it was – or about to –
        [break apart and fucking erupt]

    cause the sky was darkening,
        deafening in perpetual
    gloom
    every home i passed seemed alight with glow
everyone seemed to be cozy and safe at home

        – stranded

you were the big love of my life
fuck
i don't even know what to do now
how do i continue this narrative

***

I just lost so much hunger and fire
please let me just die in some water

      they cupped her glow
tried to snuff out her pixie dust and wonder

          they succeeded

***

the chord snapped
the guitar string struck her
in the eye
and made her bleed over her hands
flashing lights
      horrified

it is a difficult process
understanding one's own value
and what you are worth

— discordance

you haven't seen the wonders
of southeast Asia
if you have never tucked a frangipani
in your hair behind your ear
woken up to the cries of a rainforest and seen a Hornbill
or tasted *the food*
the flavours of the world
suddenly in your mouth
how it salivates
the garlic and sesame oil
watch and admire the bamboo dance
take part in it
pad around barefoot
or in flip flops at the beach
tried some ikan bilis and coconut
wait for the rain to pass
wait for hours
for days
fall asleep to the sound of thunder
it's music sometimes
they have the biggest clouds in this part of the world
clouds so big
you can't see the sky
and there's so many people
so many tanned beautiful people
young girls
hard-working girls
with large dreams

and even bigger minds

rural sentiment

modern architect

polar opposites of how their world interacts

jungle canopy

metal skyscrapers

orangutans

mobile phones

kampung houses

black and white towers

heritage buildings

a part of history

and men

men men men

just white men

existing

hierarchy and ceilings

double standards

discomfort in your own skin

there

you've soaked it in

southeast Asia

and its humidity

wipe your brow

you've finished colonising it

through the reading of these words

— southeast Asian wonders

my feelings
 can be described
as a ball of yarn
 impossible to
  untangle
 as a cat,
 just a ball of mess
only easy to look at
 and get stuck in.
 the problem
  transfixing
the only weapon I have – my claw – rendered useless

– ball of yarn

I don't know what I'm trying to say
        it's not easy.
                I think what I'm trying to say is.
introducing yourself as being
from a certain country
is hard
when the response is
I used to live there as a child
in one of those nice houses
Oh
You mean when we were colonised
Under your rule
I understand I am privileged
but your privilege is on another level
and it's strange walking around somewhere else
and enjoying museums
but realising the artefacts are stolen
products ripped from another place
the place that was meant to be mine
but isn't
the place that was conquered, subjugated, spat upon
bent to another's will
by force
it is *confusing*
how our past is
stained with a bloodied history
from clean gloved hands

how our monuments, legal systems, administration,
architectural designs
still hold true
and are just somewhat moulded into 'our own'
but what are the remnants of this
the relics and residue

I recognise street names,
and building names,
and coats of arms

can things be yours
if they didn't start as yours
how some things have changed
but others have not

– museum artefacts

i just feel

that things were looted

and we were treated

as subpar humans

we were just bargaining chips

tossed down and exchanged

over the gambling table

in the interests of others

in the back room

(whilst still being in full view)

hear the beaded curtains jingle

witness how a colour – the lack of –

an accent

a drawl

height

will get you further in life

see your people

the girls

yourself

bend to their will

like a flower leaning towards the sun

despite knowing it can sear

      and fade petal colours

                              most of the time

do we bleach ourselves
because there are so many flowers
with colours
in this part of the world
or are we bleached by
others
because it is inevitable
for it to occur

especially,
in the
tropics

here
let me serve you a drink

you look hot and bothered
how's the sun against your complexion
come inside into the shade please

there are still lingering ghosts
that haunt us

– in the back room

                    then night falls
              and the flying insects swarm
                  they hover near the light
             to escape the heat and humidity
                      only to be scorched

                            – my thoughts

I am human
I am human

why do you keep treating me as something disposable

I wish I could take the sadness out of me
Like wringing a sponge
For the water to come out

***

my last name is not altruistic
please stop expecting me   to be   it.
I am bone dry
from all
the bleeding and giving
the digging deep
and not receiving

                                           I have dug
                                           to the pits of the
well

                                           and it is empty
                                           and solemn

                                           its walls are no
longer damp with promise

                                           it's barebones and
forgotten

                                           it doesn't remember
the last time

                                         when water touched
it

and called it home to stay

                                                      – the well

***

That feeling
when you've had so much fun
and you come home
alone
kick off your heels
and suddenly you feel it
that weight on your chest
falling from such great heights
and you
         lean in on the door and
give in to
         cry

                             – it starts in the chest

***

    it only takes one word
    sometimes one action
    for everything to fall apart

You were a coward
You didn't dare
ask
Didn't dare speak
Articulate it in words
Make it more concrete
You waited for me
to voice it out
You didn't dare breathe

about
the end of our relationship
how we could have salvaged it
To prevent it from being
destroyed
You thought it was better
to sweep it under the carpet
Thought feigning it
Would transform it
into reality
but it was just cowardice

– cowardice

I thought I saw you
but then we walked past
our sleeves almost touching
but eons apart
a second later
— my afterthought —
You didn't walk that way
You had that bounce in your step
The one that was once endearing
But now looking
back
Just telling
of how you would
step on me as you did
with glee

                                 — that bounce in your step

                           ***

        he used to say my stretch marks
        were stripes on a tiger
        his words made me feel strong enough
        brave and powerful
        but in hindsight
        it's because of their coats
        that tigers are hunted

                                 — tiger stripes

we were close
then you cut me from your life
you chose her
and didn't think twice

---

you shut me in a store room
with no windows
when i broke free and ran away
you feigned outrage
it was disappointing
you thinking that i wanted to stay captive
with your false niceties
you weren't helping me
you were trapping me
with a smile

Fuck niceties
I'm done being the good girl
The nice girl (which is what most parents know me as: this
was my identity, for all three years of my previous relationship)
The submissive girl
The Asian girl

Fuck all these labels
And judgements
Wrong perceptions

I'm gonna cut you
Just as you cut me
For
Being cut
And cutting relationships
Is part and parcel of life
It's drawing boundaries
And growing up
And falling out of relationships and love

***

>Let me welcome you
>With open arms like a Rafflesia
>I emit a pungent smell
>Of rotting flesh
>Which I learnt from your habits
>As I sat there quietly in the corner
>Waiting to grow
>Biding my time
>Amongst my gnarled vines
>
>Let me capture you
>With my charm and
>Hypnotic looks
>There is no one else like me in the rainforest
>I am the Majesty,
>Royalty
>When you're scum

I will strangle you
with the full force of
a boa constrictor

My entire body one flexed muscle
ready and poised
to crush you
slowly
sweetly
taking my time
because I don't need to go anywhere
do anything else
but savour the time
that I can spend with you

***

we tore red sugar cane
from their stalks
chewed on it greedily
its sweetness trickling down our lips
our necks
leaving trails
of sugar stains
dried on our skin

– sugar cane stalks

how your association of feelings
with people
change
over time

***

And I didn't write anything for you
Because I will not grace
My words
My power
Another second for you

– not another second for you

When will

My life

Be swallowed by waves

From

The neighbouring seas and oceans

        The tidal waves plunging

Leaving me bare and

        open

                – swallowed by waves

***

Maybe I struggled so much with London
Because it was the first time I was ever away from water
The first time I could not submerge
                    underneath
                                    and swim
without its familiar embrace on my skin
like kisses from a mother
Accepting all your mistakes
and falls
slip ups and
anxieties

———

when you break up with somebody
all you want is connection
that is all

a flower kept indoors

will be unable to grow

when there is no sunlight and no one to appreciate her beauty

———

To all the lonely hearts

Refresh &

Restart

***

during summertime

everyone wears more colours

their Sunday best, only everyday

in summer,

the birds seem to chirp more

and the night is kept at bay

like a dog on a leash

the grass is fragrant

and it perfumes the air

the gardeners are wiping their brow

constantly

to keep it freshly trimmed

the Aperol and sangria a free-flow

the chatters on a whim

it buzzes the air, incessant

a free-for-all everywhere

you have waited patiently for the whole year for it

so now run along

bask in it

                        you've earned it

You looked at me
As if I was your whole world
No one had ever looked at me that way before

―――

What are all these new feelings?
I haven't felt them as an adult.
These stirrings in my belly,
The butterflies I had as a child.

―――

Your hair was tousled dark waves
A stormy night
With quiet eyes

we were beneath the cliff-faced coastline
entangled in each other's arms and sand
tucked away in a secluded cove
hidden in the bay of Broadstairs

concealed thanks to erosion
chalk cliffs left unfrequented
perfect skyline in the month of August

lights dimming
winter coming
lightning trembling in the distance

we were quiet

watching in unison

      does anyone else
           recall movies from the way
      they watched it with someone

on the couch
in the bed
in their arms
crying
or barely paying attention at all

      – memory is a peculiar thing

———

        and here I was
        reminiscing of the way
        we watched [named movie]

———

your mouth is often straightened
into a serious smile
but how I like to see it upturned for me,
with your cheeks uplifted slightly
into a softer smile

        I couldn't focus on the movie
        Not with you breathing next to me

***

How can we be forever
When we were a summer's love
With the world getting hotter
The seasons skipping
flash-forward to winter
in February
No time for autumn
leaves
Just enough time to memorise your eyes
The flecks of brown staring back at me
Shit I blinked
The moment's passed now
Didn't commit it to memory somehow
Didn't burn a hole in my brain and sear it in my mind
let me just
carve out my corneas on a platter
Take it all
Fuck

You are the summer love I want but can't last

***

Interesting how memory alters
an old man
how it can forget, mess up and rearrange

When I lived in London, I longed for the sun
When I moved, I missed the vibrancy, the grunge
the music and the streets
the architecture and the upkeep
the clothes that people wear
their attitude and flair
the theatre and sarcasm – nowhere else to be found
but most of all its age
the long rich history
freedom abound

I missed it all
even the rain
I was not used to thunderstorms any longer
I longed for
grey skies
romanticised
the soft pitter-patter on the window
barely amplified

                – memory is a shape-shifter

                    I enjoy the anonymity
                    that you get in cities

how you can be anyone you want to be
even just for a single day
and nothing would be amiss
in a place with millions of people

**

I remember seeing a guy once
cross the road
                     and fight traffic
just to get to the middle of a roundabout
                           he climbed over some trees and
plants
                  before disappearing
I know he probably went in there to take a piss
but what if it was magic?
and he went to retrieve a portkey

                                – it's the small things

Have you ever wondered why
No one stops to ask
What do you want
in life?
                for you
          to have to a full life

                              – ma chérie

***

I've started thinking about my life
in the form of opportunity cost
If I'm doing this
What else am I missing out on?

                          – opportunity cost

a hurricane of bats rose into the air
away from the columned treasures of
stalactites and stalagmites
dripping stillness
absolute chillness
even the air tastes different
60 million year-old business

life was untouched here
the water brown and blue
its jagged peaks and sunrise streaks
the harmony of noises
green jungle foliage

euphonic cacophony
a delightful novelty
the spirit full, and joyous with honesty

this was
as they say,
a complete explorer's odyssey

– Mulu caves

relying on yourself

is the best

cause it prevents the destruction of

expectation

***

like the tundra with its permafrost
when you thaw
things will start to grow again
and thrive from the cracks
like heather and cushion plants
so soft to touch and rest your cheek upon

you can be a tundra rose
or cottongrass
a labrador tea carpet
you can bloom and adapt amongst the barren rock
you can be vivid against the winter chill
you can captivate

— tundra

isn't it strange
picturing this
a swimming pool
above a carpark
infinite blue
suspended over
engines and screws
naked freedom afloat
compared to
sitting down, hunched up, bunched up inside a metallic drum

as humans
why do we always do this
make things so that everything is
compartmentalised
in cubicles
efficient
blocks
of towers
living
atop
each
other
squished
into the smallest spaces possible
in order
to prevent us
from living

our

true potential

reduce us

and restrain us

into tighter spaces

like

being constrained in the

gaps

between words

to prevent us

from being words ourselves

restrain us from

living

with purpose

and meaning

my lone chair
window
vase

it's miraculous
how objects represent feelings
without trying

our minds are so receptive
we can piece things together and assign colours to meaning
like nobody's business
the neurons and pathways and networks firing
pinging to each other like highways crossing
lights streaking
bulbs flashing
sparks
        blossoming
                behind one's eyes

our formulations
      like music compositions
of staccato and legato
         reggae and soprano

                      from a young age
              we are taught that a tree means this
                  red means anger or passion
                      blue is sadness
                we allocate our ideas and
                  section off our feelings

    we make it work somehow
    we somehow make it function
                      – pinball machine

are we meant to function
or thrive

***

life is but a social construct
malleable
yet brittle in design
ductile yet firm in its mould

its structure organised and arranged
in a meaning comprehensible to all
yet incomprehensible to some

we can tear it apart
and yet we don't
we can crumple it and toss it aside
and yet we won't

we cast this shadow
upon ourselves
tear out our hair and beat our chest
fling ourselves onto the floor
the thorough tantrums

we yearn to be awake
       [to rewrite our affairs]
       [leap forward to the sun]

but then we cover our eyes
and brush our hair
to go back to sleep

– our pillows

---

we're drones waiting to do our bidding
rats scurrying in the drain
jam-packed in rush hour
cramped bowling pins side by side
struggling not to be knocked
                      over
sat in the cubicle
lonely with our sad lunch
off to graduate
to marry
to slave
toil
and die

                      – daily commute

try again
> you've been neglecting your practice
> reassert your opinion.
>> your presence.
> you are a whole being
> act like it

                              – believe

———

your life should not have to
depend on a clock
your freedom whittled down to seconds
your day segmented
to eat, work, sleep
each minute dictating your schedule
your availability
to function

you should be boundless

outside the confines of
seasons and calendars and hours and time

of incessant tick tocks
and alarms
chasing you down

Does it get easier over time?
This thing we call adulthood

***

here's a challenge
think of your safe space
and then get yourself there

***

The only prophecy you need to
Believe in
Is that one day
You will die

Everything you have built for
Will crumble
Everyone you have loved
Will perish
Everything you know
Will change

— the only necessary prophecy

for our whole lives
we are burdened.
to work just to breathe
to accumulate to a phantom pinnacle
to then just
disperse into energy

even that is generous
other words would describe it as
dust

and nothingness

I say I love you too easily
Maybe because I want more love in this world

***

I gave it so liberally
I didn't think twice
just gave
and gave and gave
till it ran dry

– naive

If it is
as they say
that your heart is the approximate size of your fist
then why isn't it easier
to unclench it from
within your chest
just as you would unfurl your fingers
to release some sand

***

could the whole world
its women and men
couldn't we just
lift each other up
and support each other's dreams to
find our true potential

why does this feel so distant
      forgotten
                                    and far-fetched

                    the narrative of colonialism
                needs to be up for discussion more
I wonder what the trees would tell us if they could speak
                    something bona fide

***

I thought I was good at reading people
Apparently I'm not
I'm just disenfranchised

      racists should go fuck themselves

***

even an ordinary conversation can be ruined

what sort of mushrooms did you have in your stir-fry?
oh the normal ones
what, white?
yeah

let that sink in
how white is the normality

– you have so many barriers because of your skin

let me sing in bitterness with the paradox of it all

and SCREAM

***

We only die once in this lifetime
But we die a million deaths

through ignorance
and others arranging us
against
the shooting wall
the guillotine
putting us to death

***

what if you were the exception
being heterosexual

would you like being questioned
    and judged
    forced to accept peoples' discrete actions
    when you tell them
    your love preference
    a quick blink
    a smile
    why is this even up for discussion

***

[how it's like in some places]

stylish streets
manicured gardens
organised fathoms
brittle and weak
the systems, sterile
our futures in peril
melting under the wails
of broken hearts
and unspoken promises
vanishing
unbecoming futures
unravelling

all this second-guess work
your future charted
different
how can you plan a future with
someone
if there is no way
    if the structures and
pillars of society
    stand in your way
this is significant
this is deliberate
why
what a terrible, terrible
deliverance

your rights disintegrated
        into dust
how can you create a home if you're not allowed
      <u>prevented</u>
from having a family
when you are not accepted
for yourself
for who you are
it is insane
this blistering belligerence
this
nonchalant indifference

I'm sorry my love
I just want you to be free
I want you to choose
to freaking be,
something that represents you,
      effortlessly,
            truly & completely

***

when places brew something sinister
society has to stop drinking
its potion
and enchantment

***

for those of you who love men
and for those of you who love women
you're fucking phenomenal, to be who you are
to love with strength and resilience
despite the odds,
the consequences, the barriers and systems in place

it shouldn't be this way
it shouldn't be this hard
considering that we're already in the 21st century, it's a fucking joke

***

How is it so hard for some to celebrate love

it is not a crime
it is not unnatural
it is not grossly indecent

it is love
and consent
and courage to be true in a harsh world
a human right

***

thunderous applause
the cold blast of the air conditioner
feeling a bit too bare for your liking, when peeling off your
track suit bottoms
deposit them in the basket
sudden silence
repress the churning
swallow the bile
poise yourself on the starting block
slowly now
grip the edge
flex your toes
breathe in
and <u>hold.</u>
take your mark
tense and taut
the gun sounds
launch off
with as much power as possible
the stadium erupts once more
but you can't hear it
because you're
underwater

– gaze up at the lights, before the stillness

one thing I love about swimming when competing
is that the nerves and nausea
disappears
once your fingertips and head breaks the water
it's just your hands slicing
heart pounding
feet kicking
that matters

— chaos in the silence

---

give it your all
give it your breath
grit your teeth
bear the pain
cry in your goggles if you have to
lose if you must
but never
give in
never give up

toxic masculinity

I've had so many men in power
seniority
Tell me to wear makeup
Tell others to wear makeup
They appear to be decent people before – easy to get along with
and polite – and then suddenly, they – whack it in your face
One even said, I quote: "there's no such thing as ugly ladies, just lazy ladies."
WOAH BUDDY
BACK THE F OFF
he has two boys too
Can you imagine how they're being raised
How they will treat others around them because of this phrase
It makes me so angry
We are not yours to command
We are not commodities
Just fucking leave us ALONE

Who the hell do you think you are
What right do you have
The fucking audacity – the insanity
Idiotic
Mediocrity

Think of it, think!
How does he treat his wife

unconsciously berate

How does he rear his ugly head

his toxic masculinity; leaching into all rooms, the living and the bed

It sickens me to even imagine it

I cannot envision breathing it – *living with it*

Co-existing with this

The worst part is, he doesn't even see the issue:

his heedless ignorance and infantile behaviour

of course this is the case

he has his head stuck up his arse

– i'm right, they said

———

my previous male boss who told me this before

has a young daughter

I cannot imagine

how it will destroy her

bit by bit

break her down

the pursuit of shrapnel chasing her

the shards descending down

all her life – by her own father no less

through passive aggressiveness

and shallow words

– he has a young daughter

what are you putting out into this world
can you see the effects
how it ruins people's self-esteem
and makes them feel wrecked
dejected
flat out rejected
cause they're imperfect
their worth detracted
infected
the whirrings in their minds
distracted

This, this is how you make people small
it's wretched

I ran to tell my family and complained.

    My sister said, "what a fucking asshole, so dumb and ignorant"

    My mother said, "we do not have to believe him or his words/he can say whatever he wants/we do not need to accept/or fall victim to them/we don't need to feel hurt or angry/his words are just letters/like the wind that blows from one end to another/they're just vibrations"

    My dad said, "castrate him"

but the humidity was suffocating
it weighed on my chest
just to walk across the street
was like walking through water
chest deep

**

my grief
made me lose the will to live
or more importantly
save my human flesh and skin
for I had already died
long ago, long within

I'll be their Ophelia
drifting and floating,
a noblewoman even in death
a flower garland
in my hair

preserved for men
and how they like to see me as –
pretty,
youthful and in a dress

– even Ophelia was Shakespeare's

you'll be surprised
with how much
girls absorb
into their skin and minds
branded like a fire poker
pressed against
their memory

> it's always the bad ones,
> the trauma,
> i still remember moments
> from a lifetime ago

    — hot poker trauma

> wish I had Parkinson's
> so I could forget
> him
> us
> the experience

    — Parkinson's

one thing I will never take for granted

is

feeling safe in a country

but this is an

illusion

as a woman

you are never safe

not anywhere

from stares

either leering

or

friendly

you are never safe

not even from yourself

Never trust a guy
Who says he's your big brother
And then rests his hand on your thigh
In the back of a taxi

———

When I crush mangosteens
in between my two hands
I see your blood
stained in my two palms

— mangosteens

———

I wish someone would have told me
not to waste my potential
on boys

that time is precious
and that even a little time
will leave stretch marks

— I'm not your mother

how is it that
it's easier for me to breathe underwater

and into the night I toiled
the words pouring out of me
like Sept cascades falls
the Mauritian dream
Tamarind sins

I stayed awake
because I couldn't sleep

---

      you were

          a sight for sore eyes
          your open lips
          of blue and white
          the crest of your hand
          and how you waved
          from the shoreline
          how you accepted me gracefully

          grateful for my body
          when I dove in
          inside

                    – blue-lipped kiss

***

and you've come to the edge of the pier
and the mountains around the lake
are reflected cyan-green
the water is clean
but unfathomable
you feel so small
but free
and the wilderness is deafening
the water beckoning
its existence as nature
mammoth in reckoning

– Bunsen Lake

La Jonction

and I travelled alone
I leapt off the bridge
with the other teens
even though I was no longer one
I let the water carry me
all the way down
to where it meets and kisses
another river
la Rhône
to converge as
one in unison

do you realise

Humans are so resilient
we absorb pain
and forget it
like women going into labour
and then having another kid

***

everything is just feelings
don't take it so personally

most of the time
we can't do much
but why does it so often feel like a
blunder in the dark

---

my bare chest
opened wide
on the operating desk

Maybe I'll be that curveball that
came in your life
the one that slammed through
Your ship's deck and main mast
A cannonball explosion

Love should fit
like a key in a lock
the contented sigh
of a door swinging open

Love should piece together
like a jigsaw puzzle
that completes a whole picture
with its future mapped out

Love should make sense
like brushing your teeth everyday
something instinctive and natural, there's
no need for extra thoughts or proliferations

Love should grow
like a stalk in a rainforest
it's nature finding its way
winding up towards the sky
flowering when it's time, the full blossoms

Love is a feeling, a word, a commitment
Love should flow, meander and run
Love is the only thing worth chasing for on this planet

It's the best fulfilment,
a blessing under the sun

— jigsaw puzzle me this

***

the first time I felt safe in London
I nearly cried with relief and wonder
I finally felt comfortable walking
in my own skin
suddenly it felt like it was ok
to breathe
and going to the store felt
like I was taking a step into the future
something better
it wasn't just existing
or holding on

so
it was not a surprise that
when I first saw
dawn break
on my street,
the sky
lit up
in yellow, orange and pink
lavender hues like melted paint
I had tears in my eyes
and was filled with gratitude

– Maida Vale

everything is subject to change

***

and I fell asleep
to the sound of the rotating fan
whilst pretending they were
cicadas chirping
and serenading me to sleep
with the French balcony doors open
and the sea laid bare in front of me

– French balcony doors

***

hush, silence now
it's raining outside
and the rain is washing away your fears, crimes and regrets
it's washing you anew
go to sleep
and when you wake
you will be reborn

to the people
who broke your heart
thank them

they've helped make who you are
and propelled you into
the future

***

here, I kiss your brow
have courage my sweet
these blessings are endowed
for your decisions to be more complete

— goodnight kiss

***

anything related to water is romantic
walks by the canal
riverside
sea

— my memoirs

i prefer the symmetry of

mountains

rivers

and songs

how the wind beckons

as a lover would in my ear

how it plays in my outstretched fingers

as music would for a symposium

how the oceans flood

like water cupped in a giant's mouth

the grass unbidden

smitten with the dandelion

puff on the seeds

wish on the hour

without conditions

without inhibitions

without any grievances

left in this world

– my full ignition

autumn is my favourite month
I love the colours
and the crackle of leaves
I love running into the neat piles
and sending it in the air

I found a purple leaf once
and they're really rare
it was like a gift from mother nature to me
it made me feel special

how could you not
the trees are literally serenading to you
and sending you confetti
they're celebrating their end-of-life
your end-of-year party
your very own fête
in the city or countryside
your happiness in
autumntime

– a painter's playground

if you ever want to find peace
and awe
simultaneously at the same time
get yourself to the middle of a desert
and wait for nightfall
then look up
and sigh

the stars are plentiful
they glitter like nobody's business
they shine without you telling them to
and most importantly
they make you feel small
without being insignificant

— Wahiba Sands

***

love is a non-verbal knowing
an intrinsic understanding

— you just know

a Welsh love letter
>   to my link parents

your cottage by the sea
your generosity
the wine
hot meals
and love
held open arms

crumble pie with cream
warmed oven plates
board games by the fireplace
long walks in the fields and forests
let's climb the ladder to
get to the seaside together with Norris

flat stone rocks
giant's land
our afternoons free like an open hand
brunch in your breakfast nook
curled up reading first edition books
picking wild blackberries together
watching the moon smile in Cheshire
enraptured by your tales and stories
chasing sunsets and landscapes for glory

admiring how time froze
every time I returned to you
everything in leisure
the Welsh for pleasure
more adventures, together forever,
coastline walks to the lighthouse in our late Novembers
wait for me there
at Nash Point and Marcross
take me back
to crumbling walls and kissing gates
to flushed faces and card games

long days and evenings with you
let's let them melt into one before us

to whichever boy I date
        I will bring home to introduce to you

have you ever seen the sky
aflame in rainbow streaks
messy warm colours
a riot of orange and pink rising
before it softens
into muted blues and greens

I remember painting this in art class
but my art teacher didn't believe me
and gave me a D
I felt sorry for her
for never witnessing one of these sunsets
when the sky is in watercolour
paint

***

and she learnt to walk on land

In this life
or in the past life
we
would have been together

I have so much conviction
that we will be in the next

                     — I believe in the afterlife

***

the message you should always repeat to yourself is
this is your life

I have always wanted my grave to be engraved
Here lay Sheryl,
A writer

end

to you,
to anyone who wants it
and anyone who doesn't

I hope you experience a limitless love
one without bounds

Disclaimer:
All that I've written is:
a solution of truths,
fabrications
either made-believe and/or exaggerations
        of realities, or fantasies, or otherwise

If you're still wondering if it's real –
        It is.
Because it is based on emotions
that have been felt
and experienced.
        (at one point or another,
         by myself or others)

        (the world's history too long and unfathomable
        memories too many, it's unimaginable)

This book is very much a compilation of that
but remember, or at least do not forget
that feelings   and emotions don't last
no matter how much they linger

And anyways
that's not the real point
The point is to literally sit down
Have some coffee and
say hello to all my exes